KU-333-920

THE ROOTS OF
METHODISM

"*Come, O Thou that hast the seven stars in Thy right hand, . . . perfect and accomplish Thy glorious acts, . . . and as Thou didst dignify our fathers' days with many revelations above all the foregoing ages since Thou tookest the flesh; so Thou canst vouchsafe to us, though unworthy, as large a portion of Thy Spirit as Thou pleasest, . . . seeing the power of Thy grace is not passed away with the primitive times as fond and foolish men imagine, but Thy Kingdom is now at hand, and Thou standing at the door.*"

JOHN MILTON.

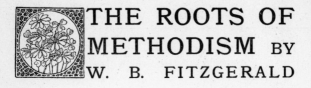

THE ROOTS OF METHODISM BY W. B. FITZGERALD

LONDON: CHARLES H. KELLY
2, CASTLE ST., CITY RD., & 26,
PATERNOSTER ROW, E.C. 1903

PREFACE

This little volume makes no pretence to original research. It is simply an attempt to explain the meaning of Methodism to the Methodists of to-day. It is an endeavour to follow the ideas and institutions of Methodism back to their roots, to trace their origin in that wonderful story of the past which is so full of inspiration for the present. Lives of Wesley and Histories of Methodism abound, but here will be found only those great outstanding facts which every Methodist ought to know, and the knowledge of which will, it is hoped, lead to that further study briefly outlined and suggested in the final chapter.

The story of our origin as a Church is full of romance, crowded with incident, and rich in heroic character; and I have endeavoured to make the old times live again in the imagination. Our Church to-day is rich in young life, and it is to be feared that very few have even a fragmentary knowledge of the reasons for the existence of Methodism. It is the feeling that such a knowledge would result in

a widespread revival of the old spirit that has led me
to attempt a task which might have been better performed by those more skilled than myself.

I am indebted to many writers, as every student
of the subject must be ; and in one chapter, " The
Faith of a Methodist," I owe some exceedingly helpful suggestions to Dr. Findlay.   In the final chapter,
"Itineraries of Thought," I have been greatly helped
by several Methodist experts, whose names will be
found in the proper place.   To the Rev. Richard
Green, known to everyone as a lover of all things
distinctively Methodist, I would also make grateful
acknowledgment for his kindness in reading the
proofs.

W. B. FITZGERALD.

HEADINGLEY, 1903.

CONTENTS

———♦———

CONTENTS

x

CONTENTS

I.

A RED LETTER DAY IN ENGLISH HISTORY

"*Now as Christian stood looking and weeping, behold three shining ones came to him, and saluted him, with 'Peace be to thee'; so the first said to him, 'Thy sins be forgiven.' The second stript him of his rags, and clothed him with change of raiment. The third also set a mark in his forehead, and gave him a Roll with a Seal upon it, which he bid him look on as he ran, and that he should give it in at the Celestial Gate; so they went their way.*"—BUNYAN.

"*Whoso hath felt the Spirit of the Highest*
  Cannot confound nor doubt Him nor deny:
Yea, with one voice, O world, though thou deniest,
  Stand thou on that side, for on this am I."
    F. W. H. MYER'S "ST. PAUL."

A RED LETTER DAY IN ENGLISH HISTORY

"It is scarcely an exaggeration to say that the scene which took place . . . forms an epoch in English history."

THESE are the words of no irresponsible scribbler, no squanderer of superlatives, no mad manufacturer of sensations, but of Mr. Lecky, the sober, fair-minded, though often rationalistic, historian of the eighteenth century.

So important does Mr. Lecky consider the event referred to, that he chronicles not only the year, but the day, the very hour when it happened; and one is curious to know what it was in his estimation, that warranted so strong a statement.

There were so many stirring events in the eighteenth century.

There was the Battle of Plassey, for instance, in 1757. Historians love to chronicle battles,—they give colour to the narrative, and this particular conflict turned the fortunes of a nation. It was no light matter for Clive, daring as he was, to advance with less than three thousand men against the fifty thousand of Surajah Dowlah, and we do not wonder that he pondered for an hour before giving the order to fight. But the result was an utter rout of the

3

enemy, and the foundations were laid of our vast Eastern empire.

But Mr. Lecky is a modern historian, and perhaps he had in his mind the victories of peace. In 1769 Watt patented his steam-engine. The steam-engine is a fit symbol of the industrial age, and its invention might fairly stand out in the philosophy of history.

Or was it that thrilling scene in 1763, when John Wilkes was sent to the Tower for daring to criticise a minister of the Crown in the columns of the *North Briton.* Wilkes himself was a worthless, profligate fellow, but he represented the *liberty of the press,* and the whole nation rose in his defence. When we think of the enormous influence of journalism in more recent times, we feel that the Wilkes' case was undoubtedly one of the events that determine a people's destiny.

And yet the sentence at the head of this chapter refers neither to Clive, nor Watt, nor Wilkes, but to a remarkable incident which took place in the life of John Wesley.

May 24th, 1738, at a quarter before nine.

That was the hour, the day, and year of this epoch-making scene, and the story of what happened is best told in Wesley's own words.

His Oxford days were over—the days of the Holy Club, the prison visiting, the rigorous discipline of devotion and service, which still left the heart unsatisfied. He had just returned from Georgia after a course of High Churchism, "beating the wind," as he himself describes it, and apparently no nearer the harbour than when he set out.

He landed in England on February 1st, and a week later was introduced to Peter Böhler, who had arrived with his little company of Moravians. The story of the Moravians must be reserved for a later chapter, for it opens out a romance of history of the very deepest interest. Wesley had already felt the influence of their simple godliness on the voyage to Georgia, and during his residence there, but the friendship with Peter Böhler was destined to be critical. Wesley helped to find him lodgings, made him known to his brother, who became Böhler's English tutor, travelled with him, argued with him, prayed with him, and soon discovered that this young Moravian—he was only twenty-five years of age—had a "peace through believing," which he himself longed to possess.

At last, on this momentous day, the great change came.

"I think it was about five this morning that I opened my Testament on these words, 'There are given unto us exceeding great and precious promises, even that ye should be partakers of the divine nature.' (2 Peter, i. 4.)

"Just as I went out I opened it again on these words, 'Thou art not far from the kingdom of God.' In the afternoon I was asked to go to St. Paul's. The anthem was, 'Out of the deep have I called unto Thee, O Lord: Lord, hear my voice.'

"In the evening I went, very unwillingly,

to a society in Aldersgate Street, where one was reading Luther's preface to the Epistle to the Romans. About a quarter before nine, while he was describing the change which God works in the heart through faith in Christ, *I felt my heart strangely warmed. I felt I did trust in Christ, Christ alone, for sal=vation. And an assurance was given me that He had taken away my sins, even mine, and saved me from the law of sin and death.*"

It is of this scene, familiar to all readers of Methodist history, that Mr. Lecky says—

"It is scarcely an exaggeration to say that the scene which took place at that humble meeting at Aldersgate Street forms an epoch in English history."

A careful study of subsequent events fully justifies the insight of our eighteenth-century historian.

When Wesley was doing the great work, which I shall endeavour to outline in later chapters, there were three rocks ahead for the English people.

The first of these was the Industrial Revolution.

During the early half of the century England was a land of green pastures and pleasant waters; but before the century closed, the great towns appeared with their tall chimneys and murky atmosphere, and the clear streams began to flow slowly, and yet more slowly, until to-day they almost stick fast in their beds. Between 1750 and 1801 the population suddenly sprang from 6,000,000 to 9,000,000, out-stripping all previous rates of increase, and the distribution entirely altered. In Gibbins' *Industrial History of England* there are two maps of England, coloured in various shades of green. The light tints mark the thinly inhabited districts, and the dark shade the denser populations. In the map which represents the early part of the century, the dark green is massed all about the basin of the Severn, with a small patch in south-east Lancashire. In the later map the whole of this southern district is light, and the dark patches have gone northward.

Coal and steam were the great factors that made for change, and the new populations clustered about the great coalfields. New industries were created, and old ones were developed. China and porcelain, iron and coal, wool and cotton goods, began to be produced in quantities unknown in the history of the country, and Lancashire and Yorkshire, Staffordshire and Northumberland, stirred with amazing activity.

It was the dawn of the inventive age. The names of Hargreaves, Arkwright, and Crompton, of Newcomen, Watt, and Brindley, were soon to be associated with the marvels of machinery and engineering. So rapidly did the migration of the people take place, so unexpected was the new tendency to mass together in large towns, and so complete was the failure of the Churches to deal with the new problem, that serious social and economical dangers were created.

A great need arose, and Methodism met that need.

It was Methodism which raised up the men—men of the people—who were able to touch these new populations as no others could. Not only did it leaven them with a living and vigorous Christianity, but in doing so it accomplished a much larger task. When the history of industrialism is fully written, it will be recognised that it has been no small part of the mission of Methodism to help the workers of England to adjust themselves to the new conditions, and to fit themselves for the popular government which we now possess.

A second peril was occasioned by the *French Revolution*. It came last in order of time, but it will be more convenient to consider it here.

Why was there no reign of terror in England? It easily might have been. There were all the elements of unrest, intense discontent, large populations ill-fed and worse educated, no adequate police force, next to no local government. The events over the water threw even our statesmen into panic. Pitt, level-headed as he was, talked of "thousands of bandits" eager for the sack of London.

It is necessary to turn to the social history of the time to learn how such fears were justified. The moral life of the nation was at its lowest ebb. Religion had ceased to be a restraint. " If one speaks of religion," said a distinguished Frenchman, " everyone begins to laugh." Bishop Butler, in weighty words, said, " It is come, I know not how, to be taken for granted by many persons that Christianity is not so much as a subject of inquiry " ; on the contrary, it was " a principal subject of mirth and ridicule." Immorality abounded in high life ;

gambling infected all classes; sport was almost wholly brutal; drunkenness was accounted no disgrace; and while the middle classes, then by no means so powerful a section of the community as now, were better than those above or below them, the lower classes were simply pagan, herded together in densely populated areas where law and order were practically unknown.

There were all the materials for a conflagration, and yet it was averted. A vast change passed over the social conditions of the people, but without any of the terrible accompaniments experienced by France.

Why, beyond a few local riots, did nothing happen? The explanation cannot be given in plainer language than that of Mr. Lecky:

" 'Peculiarly fortunate' was it that the industrial revolution should have been preceded by a religious revival, which opened a new spring of moral and religious energy among the poor, and at the same time gave a powerful impulse to the philanthropy of the rich." That revival began with the preaching of John Wesley, and was carried to the remotest corners of the land by himself and his co-workers.

There was, however, one danger which was not averted. Once in the course of the century the ship of State went right on the rocks, and the result was the *American Revolution*.

Methodism again had a great part to play.

The Colonies, as we know, revolted, and set up for themselves, with the result that a serious difficulty arose. The Church of England, "as by law estab-

lished," had no provision for such a heterodox
proceeding, and the Colonial clergy, almost to a man,
deserted their flocks and left them shepherdless.
There were none to administer the sacraments, the
sick were uncared for, the dead buried without
Christian rites.

But Methodism was already rooted on American
soil, and at the Revolution she rose in her strength.
Some loyalists there were who preferred to return to
England; even Barbara Heck, fine old saint as she
was, clung to British traditions, and went north to
Canada. But Asbury and his brave band of pioneers
cast in their lot with the new commonwealth. They
were the party of progress. All through the war
they held on bravely with their work, and when
peace came they had increased fourfold. The
period which followed was one of romantic enterprise.
The story of the "backwoods' preachers" is one of
the most inspiring in religious history.

And the debt which America owes to them has
been fully acknowledged by statesmen of modern
times. "Since the days of the Revolution," says
President Roosevelt, "not only has the Methodist
Church increased greatly in the old communities of
the thirteen original States, but it has played a
peculiar and prominent part in the pioneer growth
of our country, and has, in consequence, assumed a
position of immense importance throughout the vast
region west of the Alleghanies which has been added
to our nation since the days when the Continental
Congress first met.

"For a century after the Declaration of Independence the greatest work of our people, with the exception only of the work of self-preservation under Lincoln, was the work of the pioneers as they took possession of this continent. During that century we pushed westward from the Alleghanies to the Pacific, southward to the Gulf and the Rio Grande, and also took possession of Alaska. The work of advancing our boundary, of pushing the frontier across forest, and desert, and mountain chain, was the great typical work of our nation ; and the men who did it—the frontiersmen, the pioneers, the backwoodsmen, plainsmen, mountain men—formed a class by themselves. It was an iron task, which none but men of iron soul and iron body could do. The men who carried it to a successful conclusion had characters strong alike for good and for evil. Their rugged natures made them powers who served light or darkness with fierce intensity ; and together with heroic traits they had those evil and dreadful tendencies which are but too apt to be found in characters of heroic possibilities. Such men make the most efficient servants of the Lord if their abounding vitality and energy are directed aright ; and if misdirected, their influence is equally potent against the cause of Christianity and true civilisation. In the hard and cruel life of the border, with its grim struggle against the forbidding forces of wild nature and wilder man, there was much to pull the frontiersman down. If left to himself, without moral teaching and moral guidance, without any of the influences that tend toward the uplifting of man and the subduing of the brute within him, sad would have been his, and therefore our, fate. From this fate we have been largely rescued by the fact that, together with the rest of the pioneers went the pioneer preachers; and all honour be given to the Methodists for the great proportion of these pioneer preachers whom they furnished."

This tribute is a generous one, and it is a striking evidence of the effectiveness of Methodist teaching and organisation that the Methodist churches in the United States stand foremost among Protestant evangelical communities throughout the whole world, with a membership of 6,000,000, and not less than 20,000,000 adherents.

How many people realise these things? At three great crises in the history of the English people, Methodism was needed and was not found wanting, and the spiritual force which it represents may be traced back to the change which took place in Wesley's life in that little room in Aldersgate Street. That scene "formed an epoch," says our eighteenth-century historian; and with such high authority, strengthened by a study of the times, we are un-doubtedly right in describing May 24th, 1738, as a **red letter day in English history.**

II.

THE THREE JOHNS

" Wiclif . . . laboured to effect the revival of religious life by the restoration of simple preaching, ' a humble and homely proclamation of the gospel,' and the distribution to the people of the Word of God."

H. B. WORKMAN.

" I have preached in towns and market-places; and now I preach behind hedges, in villages, castles, fields, woods. If it were possible, I would preach on the seashore, or from a ship, as my Saviour did."

JOHN HUS.

" Sent by my Lord, on you I call;
The invitation is to ALL :
Come, all the world ; come, sinner, thou !
All things in Christ are ready now."—JOHN WESLEY.

Retrospect: The Roots of Methodism far back in the Middle Ages.

14

THE THREE JOHNS

ON the sand-dunes of our coast there grows a curious plant with a long, tapering root, purple-brown in colour, and nearly a foot in length : but beyond this, burrowing into the sand, are a multitude of hairlike fibrils, so long and so delicate, it is scarcely possible to get to the end of them.

Now the big tap-root of Methodism is undoubtedly in the eighteenth century, and there are branches which we shall trace in another chapter to the strenuous days of the Puritans, but there are also thread-like rootlets linking us in the most interesting way with the historic life of the Church in far earlier times.

One of these tough, fibrous filaments of history I purpose to follow as far back as it will take us.

The little meeting in the upper room at Aldersgate Street was a Moravian meeting. Wesley had met the Moravians before. He had wondered at their courage in the storm on the way to Georgia ; he had marked the simplicity and devotion of their character ; he had discussed faith with Peter Böhler in the halls of Oxford ; it was from them that his soul caught fire. And it is only when we understand the full significance of the part that the Moravians played in the awakening of Wesley that we realise that Methodism was no mushroom growth, no birth of a night, but a living organism deeply rooted in the religious life of the past.

In the Methodist movement an influence blossomed and bore fruit, the origin of which must be sought in the England of the fourteenth century.

Three reformers are curiously linked together by the fine threads of history.

Three Johns :—

John Wiclif, John Hus, and John Wesley.

The names suggest a thread of story intensely suggestive to all who love to get back to beginnings.

It is the year 1378. In the chapel of Lambeth Palace a great gathering of bishops, priests, and monks has assembled to try John Wiclif. What a display of lawn and purple and angry faces! "They brought them forth to their tryal, in order to their condemnation," says John Bunyan of the pilgrims in Vanity Fair. Such was the spirit of Wiclif's assessors. But the worthy men are in a difficulty. They want to pronounce him guilty. The Pope says they must. But a message has just arrived from the Princess of Wales to say they must not. The Pope or the lady? Were ever time-serving ecclesiastics in more awkward dilemma? The knot is cut, however, in unexpected fashion. In rush a pack of Londoners, indignant that the people's priest should be put to such inconvenience, and they carry him off in triumph.

How curiously the times change! In the eighteenth century there were clergy who set the mob on John

Wesley; in the fourteenth, John Wiclif was rescued by the mob from the clergy.

What was the secret of Wiclif's power?

He was a lover of the people.

Wiclif's great idea, expressed perhaps less in words than deeds, was a *Church of the people*. The Church of his day was a Church of monks, friars, and priests. The people were priest-ridden. Men became "clerics" for no other purpose than to sponge on the community, and escape lay responsibilities. Spiritual religion was dead. And for the degenerate clergy of the day Wiclif had no soft words. He boldly denounced the "emperoure bishopis," with their wealth and luxury; the friars he called "sturdy beggars"; their "letters of fraternity," supposed to convey all manner of benefits to the owners, might be "good for to cover mustard pots." But for the long-suffering, ignorant peasantry he demanded homely, heart-searching religion, the religion of the Lord's Prayer, which Christ taught His disciples, "nother in Latyn, nother in Frensche," but in the language of their everyday life.

Wiclif gave the *Bible* to the people in their own tongue. They welcomed it enthusiastically. Manuscript copies were multiplied in all directions. Farmers would give a load of hay for the privilege of reading such a copy for an hour daily. A village girl who could "recite the Ten Commandments and parts of the Epistles of St. Paul and St. Peter" was as much in request as a popular singer of to-day.

It was he, too, who instituted an order of *preachers*

for the people ; at first men actually in orders, and then, as the need increased, simple laymen. There was no nonsense about Wiclif. Like Wesley, he respected tradition so long as it seemed useful, but the moment it stood in the way of something better than itself, he went straight through it. Away went precedent when he wanted preachers. For Paul, said he, "preechide fast, and axide noo leve of Petir hereto, for he had leve of Jesus Christ."

He had magnificent leverage for this new work. Oxford was the greatest of European universities, and Wiclif was the greatest man in Oxford. Crowds of students from town and village hung upon his words, read his books, and swore by his teaching. Very soon he had a following ready for any enterprise, and he sent them into the highways and hedges.

Out into the country lanes went Wiclif's "poor priests." They

"travelled from county to county and from town to town, in certain habits, under dis= simulation of great holiness, without licence of the Holy Father the Pope, or of the ordinary of the diocese."

So said a Statute of the realm, and it was truly shocking. Without permission of Pope or bishop! But away went these itinerant preachers in their russet robes, making a pulpit of the market cross and a chapel of the village barn ; denouncing the bullying rascals in cowl and habit who prowled about the countryside with pardons, indulgences, and spurious relics, and preaching plain, homespun sermons based upon honest Scripture.

As Wiclif won the nation, so the "poor priest" won the villagers. The people believed in him. There was reality in his preaching. For, like Chaucer's poor parson of a town, in whom many have seen a portrait of the reformer himself,

> "Christe's lore and His apostles twelve
> He taught, and first he followed it himself."

Steadily the conspiracy against Wiclif deepened and strengthened. His enemies persevered, and at last secured a verdict against him. Still they dared not touch him, and the brave old man died at last among his much-loved people at Lutterworth.

"We shall be troubled no more," said the friars.

But forty years later they found out their mistake, for in 1415 there came a man to the Council of Constance, in whose soul the spirit of John Wiclif lived again.

That man was John Hus.

In those days there was much interchange of thought among the universities of Europe. They used each other's text-books; scholars travelled from one to another; students of Prague finished their studies at Oxford, and so came under the magnetic influence of the great English reformer. They were the more numerous, perhaps, because a Bohemian princess was then Queen of England. When they returned to Prague they carried with them Wiclif's books and Wiclif's ideas. In Bohemia the seed fell into prepared soil. The Bohemians had never been hearty Catholics. Greek Church traditions clung about them. Their spirit was intensely national. So when John Hus became the exponent of the thought of John Wiclif, the new teaching spread in every direction. Neither Pope nor king could arrest its progress.

Dr. Johann Loserth has settled decisively the long-debated question as to the extent of Wiclif's influence over Hus. He has proved to a demonstration that the Bohemian preacher was steeped in Wiclifite ideas. The writings of Hus are often little else but paraphrases of his English master; and, indeed, parallel columns make it abundantly plain that with sublime indifference to plagiarism Hus borrowed whole phrases, sentences, and paragraphs. He made no secret of the obligation. Four years before the Council of Constance he said—

" I and the members of our university have possessed and read these books now for twenty years."

And again, in noble tribute to Wiclif—

" I am drawn to him by the love which he has for the law of Christ, in that he maintains the truth thereof, namely, that this law cannot in any point be false."

Since things were so bad, the Pope, as a first step, ordered all Wiclif's books to be publicly burned at Prague.

Just five years later, the Council of Constance burned Hus himself, and threw his ashes into the Rhine.

And then they ordered Wiclif's bones to be dug up and burned, and *his* ashes cast into the little river Swift at Lutterworth; and, in old Thomas Fuller's words—

"As the Swift bare them into the Severn, and the Severn into the narrow seas, and they again into the ocean, thus the ashes of Wiclif is an emblem of his doctrine, which is now dispersed over the world."

And the priests said, "Two pestilent fellows, now at last we have done with both of them."

Done with them? Ah! not so easily.

A German peasant, says an old fairy tale, was greatly troubled by a lively little elf who broke his teacups, curdled his milk, and made his home in the forest generally uncomfortable. So one day he packed all his household goods on his cart, set fire to the cottage, and drove off through the pines congratulating himself, "Now I shall get rid of the mischievous young imp." And the elf poked his saucy head from behind the big bedstead on the cart, and said, "If we hadn't run away we should both of us have been burned!"

The monks burned the house, but the troublesome spirit of Hus was as much alive as ever.

At the news of his martyrdom the Bohemian people rose in great wrath, and banded themselves together in the Hussite League. To this was opposed the Catholic League, which had at its command the military resources of all Catholic Germany. Yet for nearly twenty years this brave little people held its own against the chivalry of Europe.

THE THREE JOHNS

There were many parties among the Hussites, just as in our own Puritan Revolution. I do not intend to unravel the intricacies suggested by the Utraquists, Calixtines, Taborites, Chiliasts, Picards, Orphans, or Adamites. The two first were used of Moderates, who demanded "communion in both kinds," as an outward pledge against the clericalism of Rome. The last were fanatics, who wanted to go back, not merely to primitive religion, but to primitive costume, and were speedily suppressed.

The masses of the people were represented by the Taborites, and their impetuosity soon carried more hesitating spirits along with them. In open revolt against Rome they deserted the parish churches, and gathered by thousands on the hills, to which they gave the Scripture names of Tabor, Olivet, and so on. They chose their own preachers, and the vast open-air services were conducted in the Czech language. These resembled in more points than one Wesley's open-air preaching at Kingswood and Gwennap, or the first primitive Methodist camp-meetings on Mow Cop.

Imagine the enthusiasm of the huge assembly at Tabor. Forty-two thousand were there, men, women, and children. Processions of peasants came from village after village, headed by their own priests bearing the sacramental bread and wine. As they met, they hailed one another as "brother" and "sister," and passed on, rank after rank, to the great open-air demonstration.

It was Ziska, the "blind general," who took hold

of these thronging multitudes and organised them for victory. He it was who invented the "Wagenburg," or waggon fort, a strange, moving rampart of farm waggons, linked together by chains, baffling the mounted forces that opposed them, and sheltering the brawny peasants armed with pikes, flails, and massive clubs.

It was essentially a people's movement. They demanded what Wiclif taught, and sought to give to his own countrymen—the Bible for the people, sacraments for the people, and they were determined that these things should be.

Rome at last had to confess herself defeated. The war ended in compromise, more dangerous than resistance. With peace the Moderate party became dominant, and as years rolled by, the differences from the Roman Catholic Church became less and less evident. But the heart of the people never surrendered, and out of the strife of party there slowly crystallised the Church of the United Brethren.

It is not necessary to study the religious history of Bohemia in further detail. From this point, for three centuries, the history of Wiclifite ideas is the history of the United Brethren. The conception of a people's Church never died. Kept alive, first in Bohemia, then in Moravia and Poland, and again in Germany, the tradition has been practically unbroken.

But the story has its picturesque stages.

There was the *Socialist Stage* under Peter of Chelcic. Peter was a forerunner of Count Tolstoi. His ideal was the Sermon on the Mount literally understood. He preached the doctrine of non-resistance as plainly as his nineteenth-century successor. Wealth was an iniquity, and trade, beyond the provision of necessaries, simply another form of thieving.

Out of his teaching, which, to tell the truth, was only a very logical application of some of Wiclif's principles, grew the community of Kunwald, a happy valley shut in by giant mountains, and communicating with the outside world only by a narrow gorge. Here rich and poor, citizens and peasants, learned and simple, lived together in quiet love for God and for one another, until persecution broke out and drove them, like hunted deer, to the shelter of caves and forests.

Then followed the *Organising Stage* under Lucas of Prague. He was a strong, far-seeing man, determined to rescue the movement from narrowness, and to lay deep and broad foundations for the future. Under his guidance the Church of the Brethren became the "first free Evangelical Church in Europe."

Is there a more curious incident in mediæval history than the search under Lucas for a primitive Church? Somewhere in the East, among the lands of the Bible, there must exist, he thought, some survival of apostolic times. "Then we'll find it," said he, and emissaries were sent to scour the Orient. They went to the burning East and found frozen Churches: they came home, sadder and wiser men, and discovered primitive Christianity all aglow under the glaciers and snow-peaks of the Alps. Among the Waldenses of Savoy, the disheartened travellers found a very near approach to the Church of early days. It was not their first contact with them, but it led to a closer intercourse which marked a turning-point in the history of both communities.

Another notable day in the history of the Brethren was when they first heard of the young monk of Wittenberg. Luther was a kindred spirit. They had an instinct for God-sent men. Away went their deputation to grasp the reformer's hand, and to assure him of their sympathy. Luther was deeply interested. When he read their books and documents, and particularly a treatise by Hus himself on the Church, he exclaimed, "We have all been Hussites without knowing it." This was in 1517, and from that time the two streams, like twin rivers, ran on side by side, carrying life and vigour wherever they flowed.

The next hundred years were marked by great literary activity, and rapid development of principles. In Bohemia, Moravia, and Poland the Church of the Brethren took deeper and stronger hold of the people.

But with the dawn of the seventeenth century there came the blackness of thick darkness. A henchman of the Jesuits became King of Bohemia, and the Brethren and all Protestants were doomed. Their leaders were put to death, their chapels reconsecrated for Roman Catholic worship. The altars were beaten with rods, the pulpits lashed with whips, and the walls sprinkled with holy water, to free them from the taint of heresy. The whole Protestant population was disfranchised, their marriages declared illegal, and their estates confiscated. Many of the noblest families were driven into exile. Thirty thousand burghers, with their wives and children, left the country. The peasants, such as were unable to escape, were dragooned into compliance with a ferocity only paralleled by Turkish infamy in the present century. The population dropped from three millions to one.

Still the faith of the people, the faith of Wiclif and Hus, never utterly died. It smouldered among the shepherds on the hills and the peasantry of the villages. Stories of the old days were handed down from father to son, and the children grew up with a passionate longing for freedom and truth. "O Lord, how long?" was the agonised yearning of many a saint, and yet God gave no sign.

But when the eighteenth century was young, a whisper passed from farm to farm among the Moravian hills of one whom they called the Bush Preacher. He was a shepherd whom God led by a strange and eventful path to the light of life in Christ, and in lonely copses and sheltered glens Christian David revived the old spirit of Hussite days. Once more the hymns of the Brethren, never forgotten, rang out among the hills ; and more and more boldly, in cottage and barn, the peasants gathered to read the Bible and pray. But the sleeping dogs of persecution were awake at the first echo of the old teaching. There was no place for these simple-hearted men and women in Moravia.

A strange migration took place. By moor and defile and precipitous mountain paths a little band of faithful men and women stole away by night, and arrived footsore and weary at Count Zinzendorf's estate in Saxony. Band after band of peasants followed, literally counting " all things but loss " that they might win Christ. On the bleak Hutberg there sprang up house by house the colony of Herrnhut,— " the watch of the Lord."

There the Church of the Brethren had its resurrection — the Moravian Church, as we are now accustomed to call it—and one of its most striking characteristics was its breadth and catholicity. As the years rolled on they planned a great missionary programme. They would light beacons in other lands. They saw that in even Protestant countries the people were outside the Churches, while in distant lands the heathen were untouched. They aimed at the revival of evangelical teaching, at the restoration of religion to the masses. So to England and the American colonies, as well as to the snows of Greenland and the jungles of India, the Moravian bands went forth, counting not their lives dear unto them.

It is March, 1738. Two men are pacing with earnest faces the quiet quadrangle of an Oxford college. One is the most remarkable Oxford man of his time, the other represents an influence which went out from Oxford three and a half centuries ago, and which now returns to give the initial impulse to a great people's movement. One is John Wesley, Fellow of Lincoln ; the other, Peter Böhler, the leader of the English Moravian Mission.

By a strange and wonderful providence, already referred to, Wesley met the Moravian missionaries to England on the day of their landing.

"*Tuesday, February 7th* (a day much to be remembered). At the house of Mr. Weinantz, a Dutch merchant, I met Peter Böhler, Schulius Richter, and Wensel Neiser, just then landed from Germany. Finding they had no acquaintance in England, I offered to procure them a lodging, and did so near Mr. Hutton's, where I then was. And from this time I did not willingly lose any opportunity of conversing with them while I stayed in London."—*Wesley's Journal.*

The story of Wesley's enlightenment has been told in the previous chapter. But how interesting to trace this unbroken line of succession—Wiclif, Hus, Wesley. It is not a little remarkable that the leaders of the fourteenth - century reformation and the eighteenth revival should both be Oxford men. It was from Oxford that the teaching went forth that kindled John Hus, and burned steadily on through war and persecution till the torch was carried back to the English shore. And it was at Oxford that Wesley's soul was stirred by the man who represented Wiclif's unbroken influence.

With astonishing rapidity, as we shall see, the flame spread throughout the land. And then, once more, as in Wiclif's day, the poor preachers went out into the highways and hedges. On the village green and by market cross the gospel story was told by plain men with a power which swept their rude audiences like a mighty wind. The new teaching—old, and yet ever new—was carried from town to town and village to village on a wave of song. Step by step the foundations were laid of a people's Church on a scale exceeding the wildest dreams of Wiclif and Hus. The movement took a deep and lasting hold of the industrial masses of our own country. In the United States, and the greater colonies, with a fair field and no favour, its growth has been unparalleled. And when we look back to that small beginning, and consider that Methodism to-day in its various branches numbers at least thirty millions of adherents, we can only feel that, if we are loyal to these inspiring traditions, the possibilities of the future are nobler than any achievement of the past.

III.

THE CHESS-BOARD OF HEREDITY

"The body in which we traverse the isthmus of life is not a private carriage, but a public omnibus, filled inside and out with our ancestors."

O. W. HOLMES.

"A person is a very different thing from the tendencies that have converged and focussed in him through a long line of ancestors. All these may be analysed and determined with the utmost exactitude; but when you have accomplished that stupendous task, you have not explained the man. Even granted that he is the product of these, he is still something more, something new, something different from them, something greater and more significant."

ARTHUR HOYLE.

What Methodism owes to its Founder's Puritan ancestry and Anglican training.

32

THE CHESS=BOARD OF HEREDITY

Dr. Oliver Wendell Holmes, in his *Life of Emerson*, suggests that Nature moves her pieces in the great problem of life like chessmen on a board. Sometimes qualities move straight on, descending from father to son or mother to daughter, always keeping the male or the female succession, just as the black and white bishops move diagonally on their own colours all through the game. In other instances the daughter seems to inherit the character of the father, and the son has more of his mother in him, and so it goes on in a sort of alternate series, as the two rooks move from black to white and white to black again. Occasionally a generation is skipped, and you are told how much you are like your grandfather, reminding one of the pawn's first move, when a square may be missed, and a move is taken from queen's second to queen's fourth. And, not infrequently, Nature mimics the odd move of the knight, with his one step forward and second sideways, and we see an uncle or aunt imaged in a nephew or niece, or some equally puzzling eccentricity of resemblance.

Though fanciful, the illustration is suggestive, and certainly Nature seemed to exhaust all her moves in centring in John Wesley all the finest qualities of a strong and vigorous ancestry.

Will power stands out all along the Wesley line. It is one of the fundamental qualities of the stock. They were men the world could not bend, and found it next to impossible to break.

There was Bartholomew, the Puritan, born the year after Drake died, when the tales of the old sea-dogs were ringing in the ears of every true-born Englishman. He was called in derision by his enemies "the puny parson," but his soul was as big as his stature was small. He was rector of Charmouth, on the Dorset coast, when Charles II. wanted to escape to France after the defeat at Worcester, and, but for the long prayers of the little minister, he would undoubtedly have been taken. The King and Lord Wilmot took rooms at the village inn in the characters of groom and groomsman on the way to a wedding, intending to take boat the same night. The boat never came, and while they prepared to ride away to other shelter, suspicions were aroused and word sent to the rector. But the minister was at his devotions, which none dare disturb, and before they were ended, the royal fugitive was well on his way to hiding. "If ever the King came back," said Bartholomew, "he would be certain to love long prayers; for if I had not been at that time longer than ordinary at my devotion, I would have surely snapt him."

Back the King came in good earnest in 1660, and in two years' time the strait-jacket of Uniformity was offered to the Dorset rector, and, like two thousand more, he resigned his living rather than compromise his conscience. He was an old man, and, having studied physic at Oxford, he spent his last days at Charmouth, caring for the bodies, as formerly he had cared for the souls of the parishioners.

And then there was John Wesley the first, the grandfather of the one we know so well. He, like his father, was a Puritan, and a minister; and he, too, was ejected from his living on St. Bartholomew's Day, 1662. He was at Oxford in those great old days when John Owen was vice-chancellor, and Thomas Goodwin, Edmund Staunton, and John Howe were heads of colleges; and when William Penn, Philip Henry, and Christopher Wren were undergraduates. He had no episcopal ordination, but he satisfied the requirements of Cromwell's Triers, and so obtained a living.

But trouble was in store for him at the Restoration. The little village of Winterborn, Whitchurch, was in the diocese of Bristol, and the newly appointed bishop soon wanted to know why the Liturgy was not used by the young clergyman, and if, in fact, he had any right to be a clergyman at all. A long conversation with the bishop, recorded in the young minister's diary, shows that he possessed plenty of the clear-headed, common-sense, reasoning faculty, which came out so vigorously in his more famous grandson. The bishop could make no impression, and indeed he himself seems to have been the one impressed, for he let Wesley alone. But others were not so kindly, and before the Act of Uniformity was passed he was thrown into prison for the non-use of the Liturgy.

His courage and honesty came out once more in his trial.

"Call Mr. Meech," said the judge, after vainly trying to get Wesley to commit himself. "Does Mr. Wesley read the Common Prayer yet?" "May it please your Lordship," said Meech, who knew the man, **"He never did, and he never will."** The prophecy was a true one. Turned out of his rectory, he continued to preach in village and hamlet, now helping Joseph Alleine at Taunton, now living in retirement in a small village near Weymouth, and finally settling down as pastor of a Nonconformist church at Poole. But there was no peace. His meetings were broken up as conventicles; he lived in daily fear of imprisonment; for three months he lay in Dorchester Gaol, and in the prison at Poole for half a year. For months together he was hunted from cover to cover, his wife and children and flock left to themselves. But to silence him was impossible, and one is reminded again and again of the invincible will which in a later day defied all the persecutions of the eighteenth century. The heroic minister died in 1678, worn out too soon by the hardships and privations of an intolerant age.

The brave Nonconformist of Poole left behind him two sons. One, Matthew Wesley, became a doctor of some popularity in London; and the other, Samuel, became a clergyman, and, eventually, rector of Epworth.

Samuel broke with all the old Puritan traditions. In character he resembled in many points both father and grandfather ; but in ecclesiastical opinion they were at opposite poles. He became a stalwart up-holder of rule and rubric, a believer in Episcopacy and Apostolical Succession, and an opponent of Dissent in all its forms ; and yet his life was not without its elements of heroism.

Several influences contributed to his complete change of front. In his youth he was thrown among Dissenters of a peculiarly aggressive type. In the circles where he moved the lofty spirit of the old Puritans had given place to a petulant, lampooning temper, which could not long satisfy a young man of honest convictions ; and deep-seated in his own nature was an instinct for law and order which made the Establishment attractive. Led to study the question for himself, he resolved to abandon Nonconformity and to take Orders.

By this decisive step he cut himself loose from all his old friends, and, as yet, had not a single acquaint-ance in the Church of England. With forty-five shillings in his pocket he entered himself as a poor scholar at Exeter College, Oxford, and by indomitable perseverance and industry not only obtained an honourable degree, but left the university seven pounds fifteen shillings richer than when he entered it. The only financial help he received from friends amounted to five shillings.

In Samuel Wesley we begin to recognise other qualities which were prominent in his more famous son. He was a scholar and a poet. Some of his literary work received even royal recognition. His poetry was mostly the dull, passionless, uninspiring rhymed verse of the time. He spoke of himself humorously as one of those

> "Who for their own, or some forefather's crime
> Are doomed to wear their days in beating rhyme."

And yet, if a poet takes rank from his highest creation, the author of the Crucifixion hymn

> "Behold the Saviour of mankind
> Nailed to the shameful tree,"

will hold an honourable place among our noblest hymnologists.

A good story illustrates both the humour and the frankness which were equally characteristic of the son. While rector of Epworth, Samuel Wesley was once asked to dinner at the house of a miserly old man who had never been known to launch out into such liberality before. Dinner over, the rector was invited to return thanks, which he did in the following extemporaneous verse :—

> "Thanks for this feast, for 'tis no less
> Than eating manna in the wilderness.
> There meagre famine bears controlless sway,
> And ever drives each fainting wretch away :
> Yet here :—Oh, how beyond a saint's belief !—
> We've seen the glories of a chine of beef !
> Here chimneys smoked which never smoked before,
> And we have dined, where we shall dine no more."

"No," growled the eccentric host, as the last line was uttered, "No, gentlemen ; it is too expensive."

No reference to Samuel Wesley would be even fair which failed to recognise the indomitable courage, the inflexible faithfulness, the resolute pertinacity of his pastorate at Epworth. He was a preacher of righteousness among an almost semi-barbarous people. He was surrounded by enemies. His income, small enough for the necessities of a numerous family, was sadly diminished by incendiaries who burned his flax and twice fired the parsonage, reducing him at one time to practical beggary. He was flung into Lincoln Castle for debt, the consequence of disaster. Yet he showed no malice, relaxed no effort, and worked ever for truth and purity of life.

Abraham Mendelssohn, the banker, of Berlin, whose father was Moses Mendelssohn, a thinker of European fame, and whose son Felix Mendelssohn Bartholdy won immortal honour as one of the world's greatest composers, used to say, when his boy was becoming famous, "I used to be known as the son of my father, but now I am known as the father of my son."

Samuel Wesley deserves to be remembered for his own sake ; he would have a still further claim because of his Puritan ancestry ; but his supreme title to fame is the fact that he was the father of the founder of Methodism. He died four years before the Great Revival.

It has been difficult to speak of the rector of Epworth without mention of Susannah Wesley, his courageous partner through all his difficulties and hardships. With her another new force seems to come into the Wesley character.

THE CHESS-BOARD

Susannah Wesley is one of the world's great women. Her influence in shaping Methodism can hardly be overestimated. An old Spanish proverb says, "an ounce of mother is worth a pound of clergy," and the mother-power that helped to form John Wesley's character was more influential than all the tendencies inherited from divines, either Puritan or Anglican.

She was a woman of clear judgment and strong common sense, transparently sincere, not demonstrative in affection, and both venerated and loved by the numerous tribe which she brought up with almost Spartan severity.

It is not a little remarkable that she, like her husband, was of Nonconformist origin. Her father, Dr. Annesley, had a church in London. Her grandfather on the mother's side, John White, was a barrister, and so thorough-going a Puritan, that, during the Commonwealth, he was Chairman of the Committee of Religion, and one of the Westminster Assembly of Divines. Medical skill and poetic genius we have already found strongly developed in the Wesleys, and perhaps to this Puritan lawyer may be traced some of the legal acumen which was illustrated so strikingly in John Wesley's provision for the future of the Methodist societies.

But Puritan tradition and environment were burned through by the strong acids of a mind capable of thinking for itself, and which the Nonconformity of the time failed to satisfy.

A few years before her marriage she changed her views of Church government, and accepted those of the Anglican Church, in whose communion she henceforward lived and died.

She possessed an extraordinary power of will. In fact, the two dominant wills in the Epworth rectory were too strong for mutual comfort, and sometimes came into serious collision. John Wesley himself is authority for the story that his mother refused to say "Amen" to the prayer for the king, on the ground that she did not believe the Prince of Orange to be her rightful monarch. The rector roundly declared that if they were to have two kings they must part. And as Mrs. Wesley was "inflexible," part they did for twelve months, until the death of William III., and the accession of Anne, whose claims both were prepared to admit, gave an opening for reconciliation. Such obstinacy is not exactly admirable, though one is reminded of the "He never did, and he never will," when the rector's father was before the magistrates.

There are other instances where the quiet, "inflexible," purposeful spirit of the mother of the Wesleys awakens nothing but admiration.

One of the most interesting incidents in the Epworth record is the story of Mrs. Wesley's services in the rectory kitchen. Mr. Wesley was in London on ecclesiastical business, and the curate left in charge to take his work was apparently a failure. The people were being spiritually starved, and Mrs. Wesley, anxious about her own household, gathered them together, children and servants, for a homely little service. Then the farm-boy told his parents, who begged to be allowed to come. The door once opened, others followed, one after another, until the little congregation numbered two hundred.

But the mind of Mr. Wesley was disturbed, for in his eyes it was a conventicle, and the irregularity all the greater because the meeting was conducted by a woman. Mrs. Wesley's very beautiful letter telling how it all came about was not sufficient to overcome his scruples, especially as the curate was evidently annoyed by the want of appreciation of his own ministry. Mrs. Wesley wrote again, and her last words of appeal to her husband are full of character:—

"If you do, after all, think fit to dissolve this assembly, do not tell me you desire me to do it, for that will not satisfy my conscience; but send me your positive command, in such full and express terms as may absolve me from all guilt and punishment for neglecting this opportunity of doing good, when you and I shall appear before the great and awful tribunal of our Lord Jesus Christ."

It is not difficult to recognise in those noble words the spirit which was responsible in Susannah Wesley's son for the daring innovations of the Great Revival.

The same unswerving force of will makes itself evident in the training of her children.

"I wonder at your patience," the rector once said. "You have told that child twenty times the same thing." "Had I satisfied myself," the mother replied, "by mentioning the matter only nineteen times, I should have lost my labour. You see it was the twentieth time that crowned the whole."

Susannah Wesley was the first *Methodist*. Read the long and deeply interesting letter to John Wesley from his mother in 1732, explaining her principles of education, and it is clear at a glance how Methodism became possible. Some of the mightiest forces that went to the making of Methodism were inherited by Wesley from his mother, and were deepened and strengthened in his own soul by his earliest training.

Yet Mrs. Wesley had a very modest estimate of her own abilities. There is exquisite pathos in her words to her own husband in the letter previously referred to :—

"I never durst positively presume to hope that God would make use of me as an instrument in doing good. The farthest I ever durst go was, 'It may be ; who can tell ? With God all things are possible : I will resign myself to Him'; or, as George Herbert better expresses it,—

> 'Only, since God doth often vessels make
> Of lowly matter for high uses meet,
>   I throw me at His feet ;
> There will I lie until my Maker seek
> For some *mean stuff* whereon to show His skill :
>   Then is *my* time.'"

There is the beauty of unconscious holiness in the soul which these sentences unveil.

Such, then, were some of the influences that shaped John Wesley. It took both the Revolution and the Restoration to make him. Both Puritanism and Episcopacy meet in him as in a single focus. From father and mother alike he inherited a love of order and method, a respect for established authority, the instinct of patriotism and conformity. But behind these nearer influences there was the virile strength of the men of the Commonwealth, men of steady purpose and unconquerable spirit.

And out of the mill of heredity came a man, a personality, a new and original force, which impressed its own stamp on the eighteenth century, and altered the currents of history for all time. Puritan, preacher, lawyer, scholar, physician, poet,—each of his ancestors contributed some potent element of character; but the John Wesley whom we have to study was more than the sum of them, and different from all of them, a man with a great individuality,—a "man sent from God."

IV.

LIFE IN A COUNTRY PARSONAGE

"The time comes when the mother is no longer the centre and sun of the child's world; but he is no true man who, having been endowed with the priceless book of a good mother, can forget his immeasurable debt to her."—*"AENIGMÆ VITÆ."*

The early years of John Wesley in the home at Epworth. From 1703 to 1720, when he left the Charterhouse.

LIFE IN A COUNTRY PARSONAGE

A CURIOUS searcher, looking for dawning genius, would hardly have expected to find it in a small and obscure village in a low-lying fen country. Natural scenery unquestionably plays some part in the shaping of character. The men of the hills differ from the men of the plain, and the children of the sunny south are widely separated in temperament from the sons of the bleak and rugged north. But genius seems often to ignore environment, just as an erratic mineral-laden spring here paints the rocks on some wild mountain side with a coat of many colours, and here stains the soil of some lowland level with its red and orange encrustations.

Certainly there might seem little in the fen-lands to feed the imagination and stir the soul of a lad of parts, and yet from the fens came men of such varied power as George Fox, the Quaker; Isaac Newton, the philosopher; Tennyson, the most musical of poets; as well as the great religious leader who is the subject of these studies.

Epworth lies about the centre of the Isle of Axholme, a sort of delta enclosed by the Trent and Don and their tributaries, a fertile stretch of country, made still more fertile by a process called "warping," by which the low ground is flooded so that it may be enriched by the black alluvial sediment left by the retreating waters. The people in Wesley's day were rough and turbulent, but lovers of the soil. "Many work like negroes," said Arthur Young, the agricultural expert of the eighteenth century, "and do not live as well as the inhabitants of the poorhouse ; but all is made amends for by possessing land." Of their barbarity and rudeness the Wesley family had not a few experiences.

The old Epworth rectory in which John Wesley was born in 1703 was a very primitive structure. The roof was of thatch, and underneath were three low storeys—"Kitchen, hall, parlour, butterie, and three large upper rooms, and some others of common use." A little garden, a barn, a dove-cot, and a hemp-kiln, completed the little property—together with the church lands where the rector grew his crops.

We never entirely get away from the influences of childhood. There are events that grip the soul with a power never to be outgrown. Such an event in Wesley's life was the burning of the old rectory one wild February night when he was only six years old. Kneeling on the old chest at the window, leaning out of the little casement to get air to breathe, a crackling furnace of smoke and flame behind him, and without, a strange world full of piteous cries and lit up with a terrifying red glare,—it was a scene never to be erased from memory. Long years afterwards, when one of his portraits was engraved, Wesley had a tiny vignette of a burning house added below, with the words, "Is not this a brand plucked from the burning?" A life so spared was in the deepest sense a consecrated life.

The old wood and thatch burned like tinder, and little was saved, but among the few treasures discovered among the blackened ruins were two scorched slips of paper. One was a fragment of a Polyglot Bible, bearing the words, "Vade ; vende omnia quae habes, et attolle crucem, et sequere me,"—" Go ; sell all that thou hast, and take up thy cross, and follow Me." The other was the manuscript of the rector's own hymn—

> "Behold the Saviour of mankind
> Nailed to the shameful tree ;
> How vast the love that Him inclined
> To bleed and die for thee ! "

But Epworth suggests other and lighter memories. John Wesley was one of a gay, witty, active-minded family, a little world in themselves, and no doubt keen to mark any points of interest in the larger world outside.

As a boy he might remember the wrathful rector, his face ablaze with scorn, dragging the corn-thief, caught in the act, into the open market-place, and compelling him to turn out his corn-bulged pockets before the eyes of his neighbours ; who, it is to be feared, were readier to ridicule the parson than to condemn the culprit.

How his humour would fasten upon some of the scenes in church, and not least the odd spectacle of the old parish clerk, droning out the psalms from the depths of one of his father's cast-off wigs. And how the whole tribe in the parsonage pew would enjoy the situation, when, on one memorable Sunday, when the rector lined out the words of the old metrical version,

"Like to an own in any ivy bush,"—

the clerk, peering out of the big, ill-fitting wig, most appropriately responded with the next line—

"That rueful thing am I."

The version in Sternhold and Hopkins is not quite so pointedly expressed, but the story was told by Charles Wesley as above.

John was argumentative as a child. He wanted a reason for everything, and no doubt made himself a nuisance to everybody at times. Many a hasty word provoked by his combativeness would be forgotten; but among the indelible memories was a day when the rector turned sharply upon him and said, "Child, you think to carry everything by dint of argument; but you will find how very little is ever done in the world by close reason." "Very little indeed" is John Wesley's comment on the incident in later years.

But these scattered incidents only touch the surface of a home life rich in formative influences. Mrs. Wesley had definite ideas about education, and she carried them out with thoroughness. Her letter to her son John, written at his request, and outlining her system, is a most interesting document, and deserves to be studied as a whole.

Her household was a little kingdom. Obedience was its cornerstone. The tiniest children were taught to "cry softly," if cry they must; and, among the older boys and girls, loudness and rude behaviour were strictly forbidden.

The perfect gentlemanliness and exquisite courtesy which characterised John Wesley in after life, had their origin in a code of manners to which all had to submit. The will of the children, strong enough as time gave evidence, was not broken, but conquered. They got nothing they cried for, and were taught to "speak handsomely" for what they wanted. They had to eat what was set before them without question, and the order of the house was three meals a day and nothing between meals.

Some of the standing bye-laws of the household were altogether admirable.

No child was ever whipped who confessed to a fault and promised to amend. Never was a child whipped twice for the same fault, or upbraided with it afterwards.

Obedience, especially when it was hard to obey, was always commended. "If any child performed an act of obedience, or did anything with an intention to please, though the performance was not well, yet the obedience and intention should be kindly accepted, and the child with sweetness directed how to do better for the future."

Rights of property were rigidly respected as between the children even in the smallest matters, and no child was ever permitted to take what belonged to another, even if it were but a farthing or a pin. Promises were absolutely sacred.

For nearly eleven years John Wesley lived in this atmosphere, breathing day by day its spirit of truthfulness, sincerity, and justice, doing the same things over and over again until they became a part of himself. No wonder that, as a man, he became one of the most open-minded, transparently sincere, and supremely capable men of his day. He knew how to command, because he had learned to obey.

But with Wesley, as with most boys, there came a testing time. At thirteen years of age he was sent to school at the Charterhouse, and made his first plunge into the big world outside. In some country waggon he would be driven through fields and over open country (for roads near Epworth there were none), until they reached the Great North Road, and took the stage coach up to town ; and one can imagine the excitement of the boy as the sights and sounds of the busy city broke upon him for the first time.

Of his life at the Charterhouse there is little to record. A few traditions survive, but they have small bearing upon the making of the man.

One thing is certain, that in the new world of school he tasted of the tree of knowledge of good and evil, and for a time became careless and negligent in religion. But the fact that in after life he could look back upon his schooldays "not only without bitterness, but with pleasure," is evidence enough to show that he never got very far astray from the strong influences of the Epworth home.

V.

A GREAT SEAT OF LEARNING

" Beautiful city ! so venerable, so lovely, so unravaged by the fierce intellectual life of our century, so serene !

'There are our young barbarians all at play !'

And yet, steeped in sentiment as she lies, spreading her gardens to the moonlight, and whispering from her towers the last enchantments of the Middle Age, who will deny that Oxford, by her ineffable charm, keeps ever calling us nearer to the true goal of all of us, to the ideal, to perfection . . ."

MATTHEW ARNOLD,
" Essays in Criticism."

Life at Oxford from 1720 to 1735. In that year made Fellow of Lincoln. Returns after a brief absence, and joins the Holy Club in 1729. Sails for Georgia in 1735.

A GREAT SEAT OF LEARNING

A FEW years before Wesley went to Oxford there came a youth to the university, Nicholas Amhurst by name, whose career contrasts curiously with that of the Methodist leader.

Both came from great public schools; both had enjoyed the advantages of a good home training; both possessed something of the reforming instinct; and both found much that needed reform. But the evils which stirred the one to noble endeavour, poisoned and corrupted the other.

Nicholas Amhurst, like Wesley, was shocked with the unrealities and hypocrisies of the new world in which he found himself, but instead of bravely holding his own, he basely capitulated and sank to an even lower level than the men he condemned. Finding his tutors indifferent to him, and the heads of houses in some instances but sorry examples to the youth under their charge, he abandoned religion altogether, plunged recklessly into all kinds of excess, and eventually was sent down in disgrace. He ended his life in Grub Street, a clever and satirical journalist; and terrible is his indictment against the university where his own life was utterly wrecked.

His bitter letter to Dr. Delaune, the vice-chancellor,

is pathetic as a picture of the terrible disillusion which must have awaited many another in those days when the morals of Oxford were at their lowest.

"I came to your college a raw, ignorant schoolboy, and foolishly thought mankind in earnest in what they professed : I took liberty for a *real* blessing, and religion for the *real* worship of God ; I often remember how scrupulous I was in the most common concerns of life ; with what awful dread I took an oath, and with what tremendous veneration I received the Sacrament ; but how much improved I am for the better since, let my worst enemies bear witness ! ! "— (Jeaffreson's *Annals of Oxford*, p. 248.)

But the evil influences which soured and spoiled the life of Nicholas Amhurst were turned by Wesley into stepping-stones to higher things. He entered the university a gay, vivacious, intelligent youth, fresh from the Charterhouse ; he left it the most earnest man in England.

But we have ample evidence that Nicholas Amhurst's bitter words were fully justified.

Gibbon, the historian, writing of a period only a few years later, satirically describes one of his tutors as a man who " remembered that he had a salary to receive, and forgot that he had a duty to perform." Another, " one of the best of the tribe, . . . was satisfied, like his fellows, with the slight and super- ficial discharge of an important trust." At first Gibbon attended the lectures of this easy-going pro- fessor with conscientious regularity, but finding them "equally devoid of profit and pleasure," he one day tried the experiment of an apology for absence. It was "accepted with a smile." Very soon the attendance became the exception and the absence the rule, but his tutor seemed blissfully unconscious whether he came or stayed away! No wonder Gibbon described his university days as "the most idle and unprofitable period of his life."

Adam Smith, in his *Wealth of Nations*, speaking of Oxford during the years when Methodism was becoming a power in the land, uses language even more sweeping.

"In the University of Oxford the greater part of the professors have for these many years given up even the pretence of teaching. The discipline is in general contrived not for the benefit of the students, but for the interest, or, more properly speaking, the ease of the masters."

As Miss Wedgewood very forcibly expresses it: "While the student lounged away his time in the coffee-house and the tavern, while the dice-box provided him with a serious pursuit and the bottle a relaxation, he was called upon at every successive step to his degree to take a solemn oath of observance of the academical statutes, which his behaviour infringed in every particular. While the professors received £100 or £200 a year for giving no lectures, the candidates for degrees were obliged *to ask and pay for a dispensation for not having attended the lectures that never were given.*"

"Religion," says John Richard Green in his *Oxford*

Studies, "had dwindled to a roll-call," and education was "found anywhere but in the lecture-room."

But to see Oxford as it was in the eighteenth century we must look through John Wesley's eyes. Years later, when the evangelical revival was at its height, he preached in the university pulpit, and with burning words denounced the life of the university as he himself had known it in early manhood.

Let us try to picture the scene.

It is St. Bartholomew's Day, August 24th, 1744, the day when Bartholomew Wesley and John Wesley, the Puritan ancestors of the founder of Methodism, both distinguished Oxford men, were ejected from their livings. And now the inheritor of their courage and spirit, a Fellow of Lincoln, preaches in St. Mary's. Down the aisle of the famous old church move in stately procession all the dignitaries of the university,—first the beadles carrying the vice-chancellor's insignia of office, then the vice-chancellor himself, and behind him a little clergyman, decidedly under the average height, and yet a man who at once attracts the eyes of those about him. A young undergraduate, afterwards a famous Hebrew scholar, looks down from the gallery and feels that he is in the presence of a strong individuality. "His black hair, quite smooth and parted very exactly, added to a peculiar composure in his countenance, showed him to be no ordinary man."

Following the preacher are the proctors and doctors of divinity, and as these take their places the preacher ascends the pulpit, reads the quaint bidding prayer, and very quietly and slowly announces his text.

"And they were all filled with the Holy Ghost."

The sermon opens with a beautiful description of primitive Christianity, but as the preacher goes on to apply this early teaching to university life, a hush falls upon the congregation. Some of the heads of houses stand up, leaning forward as though they would not miss a single word. Seldom have weightier words fallen from St. Mary's pulpit. One can imagine the sea of upturned faces, swept by amazement, anger, shame, resentment, as the bold indictment is developed.

"What example is set us by those who enjoy the beneficence of our forefathers? by Fellows, Students, Scholars, more especially those who are of some rank and eminence? Do ye, brethren, abound in the fruits of the Spirit, in holiness of mind, in self-denial and mortification, in seriousness and composure of spirit, in patience, meekness, sobriety, temperance; and in unwearied restless endeavours to do good to all men? Is this the general character of Fellows of colleges? I fear it is not. Rather have not pride and haughtiness, impatience and peevishness, sloth and indolence, gluttony and sensuality been objected to us, perhaps not always by our enemies, nor wholly without ground? . . . Once more: What shall we say of the youth of this place? Have you either the form or the power of Christian godliness? Are you diligent in your easy business, pursuing your studies with all your strength? Do you redeem the time, crowding as much work into every day as it can contain? Rather, are ye not conscious that you waste day after day either in reading what has no tendency to Christianity, or in gaming, or in—you know not what? Are you better managers of your fortune than of your time? Do you take care to owe no man anything? Do you know how to possess your bodies in sanctification and honour? Are no drunkenness and uncleanness found among you? Yea, are there not many of you who glory in your shame? Are there not a multitude of you that are forsworn? I fear, a swiftly increasing multitude. Be not surprised, brethren—before God and this congregation I own myself to have been of the number solemnly swearing to observe all those customs which I then knew nothing of, and all those statutes which I did not so much as read over, either then, or for a long time afterwards. What is perjury, if this is not? But if it be, oh, what a weight of sin, yea, sin of no common dye, lieth upon us! And doth not the Most High regard it?

" May it not be a consequence of this that so many of you are a generation of triflers with God, with one another, and your own souls? Who of you is, in any degree, acquainted with the work of the Spirit, His supernatural work in the souls of men? Can you bear, unless now and then in a church, any talk of the Holy Ghost? Would you not take it for granted if anyone began such a conversation, that it was hypocrisy or enthusiasm? In the name of the Lord God Almighty I ask, What religion are ye of?"

It is a startling deliverance, and as the preacher

descends from the pulpit, and is joined by his brother and one or two friends, they go out alone. They are marked men. Never again will that voice be heard in the university church. And yet it was a true indictment, as the impartial witnesses already quoted bear ample testimony.

But we must go back to Wesley in his undergraduate days.

With all its faults Oxford has to be reckoned as a definite factor in the making of Wesley. It set its stamp upon the whole man. The spirit of the place took possession of him. For the famous old city has a marvellous fascination. In springtime when the foliage is at its greenest, or in autumn when the creepers are aflame with crimson, and the gold of sundown touches the mullioned traceries and steals into college halls, there is an irresistible magic about the place.

It is a city of inspiring traditions. In earlier centuries it was almost cosmopolitan. Students flocked to its colleges from all parts of Europe. It opened its doors to the poorest. It was a university in the broadest sense, and not merely an aristocratic club or High Church preserve.

Wesley caught something of the glow of these old memories. Oxford stood with him, not merely for scholarship and culture, but for the liberality which seeks to give of these to the people. We shall miss something of the genius of Methodism if we fail to realise how, in after years, this son of Oxford sought to bring the purest of literature and the finest products of scholarly genius within the reach of the multitudes who were lifted by the evangelical revival out of the slough of semi-barbarism. And, in the New World at least, the same spirit has found fine expression in the Methodist colleges and universities of the United States, where the poorest lad is welcome, and where the endowments and privileges and equipment rival, in some instances, the richest of the old Oxford foundations. Methodism was born in a university, and the evangelism of to-day must not forget that it has a mission of culture.

Wesley entered Oxford in 1720. He took his Bachelor's degree in 1724. The next year he was made Fellow of Lincoln. After two years' residence he returned home for a time to act as curate to his father, whose health was rapidly declining; but he returned to Oxford in 1729, and remained, save for short absences, until he went to Georgia in 1735.

His years at Oxford divide themselves into three periods: in the first he was the vivacious student; in the second a sombre mystic; and in the third the energetic Methodist.

The first period includes the years at Christchurch from 1720 to 1725.

A contemporary of Wesley during these early years cleverly and graphically pictures him as a "very sensible and acute collegian, baffling every man by the subtleties of logic, and laughing at them for being so easily routed; a young fellow of the finest classical taste, of the most liberal and manly sentiments; gay and sprightly, with a turn for wit and humour."

It is an attractive portrait, and, indeed, of this period little more need be said. Wesley studied hard, and at the same time entered with zest into the lighter side of undergraduate life. Neither he nor his brother ever had the slightest sympathy with the coarser indulgences which proved the ruin of men like Nicholas Amhurst. Probably few made such good use of their time. There were not many like Chaucer's "Clerke of Oxenford" who "spent all on books and learning," and John Wesley had little to spend. What little he had went freely, and he was sometimes in debt, and the home letters of the time show that it was no easy matter to find the minimum required for his university expenses.

But there were influences at work turning Wesley's thoughts towards serious things. There is a story of the time which is more than a little suggestive. Returning late one night to his college, Wesley indulged in some merry chaff at the expense of the college porter.

"Go home and get another coat," said he.

"This is the only one I have in the world," replied the porter, "and I thank God for it."

"Go home and get your supper then," said Wesley.

"I have had nothing but a drink of water to-day, and I thank God for that," was the rejoinder.

"It is late, and you will be locked out, and then what will you have to thank God for?"

"I will thank Him for the dry stones to lie on."

63

"John," said Wesley, "you thank God when you have nothing to wear, nothing to eat, and no bed to lie upon; what else do you thank Him for?"

"I thank Him," said the porter, "that He has given me my life and being, a heart to love Him, and a desire to serve Him."

A passing incident, but it left a deep impression. John Wesley felt that this humble man had found something in religion which he as yet did not possess. This, and the deeper influence of his mother's letters led the young undergraduate to give himself wholly to the religious life, and to take orders as a clergyman of the Church of England.

The next four years, from 1725 to 1729, are among the most important of Wesley's life. They witnessed great changes of thought and character, and seeds were sown, the fruit of which is seen in after years. He became a mystic, and, for the time, of a very sombre hue.

Three books had a share in his development: the *Imitation of Christ*, Jeremy Taylor's *Holy Living and Holy Dying*, and Law's *Serious Call to a Devout and Holy Life*.

The *Imitation*, with its "lasting record of human needs and human consolations," deeply stirred Wesley's spirit, though he felt its imperfections. There are three great factors in religion; God, the soul of man, and the world without. In the *Imitation*, God and the soul are throbbing realities, but the world with all its needs is forgotten. Its keynote is devotion, not service. And yet there are sentences, pulsating with emotion, which must have moved Wesley to the very depths of his nature.

"Why wilt thou defer thy good purpose from day to day? Arise, and begin this very instant, and say, 'Now is the time to be doing, now is the time to be stirring, now is the time to amend myself.'"

"Thou must pass through fire and water, before thou canst come to a place of refreshment."

"Unless thou dost earnestly force thyself, thou shalt never get the victory over sin."

Jeremy Taylor, who had "devotion enough for a cloister, learning enough for a university, and wit enough for a college of *virtuosi*," as a contemporary said after his death,—is largely responsible for the strong High Church bent given to Wesley's early career. Anti-Calvinist, anti-Puritan, advocating high sacramental doctrine with immense ardour, extravagant in his view of baptismal regeneration, and holding extreme views of the Lord's Supper, he appealed strongly to Wesley's sympathies as they had taken form at the time. It was this book that brought decision. "I resolved," said Wesley, "to dedicate all my life to God."

This resolute purpose was still further deepened by the influence of William Law, who is certainly one of the most remarkable men of the time. The eighteenth century had little enthusiasm, and more than anything else discountenanced anything like intensity in religion. Yet Law was a mystic of the mystics. He seems utterly out of harmony with his environment. As Canon Overton says, "To come across such a man in the midst of his surroundings is like coming across an old Gothic cathedral, with its air of calm grandeur and mellowed beauty, in the midst of the staring red brick buildings of a brand-new manufacturing town."

His *Serious Call* was pronounced to be a masterpiece by men so eminent and so different as Gibbon, Doddridge, and Dr. Johnson. It is a curious fact that he lived for some time in Gibbon's father's house, and Dr. Johnson said that the *Serious Call* was the first book that made him in earnest about religion.

The central teaching of the book may be summed up in a sentence from its pages.

" Nothing godly can be alive in us but what has *all* its life from the Spirit of God, living and breathing in us."

The profound spiritual truth expressed in these words had a vital influence on the teaching of the Great Revival.

During these fruitful years, Wesley was not only gaining, but losing. It was in 1725 that he finally flung away the old husk of Predestinarianism. Calvinism, in its narrowest signification, was preached everywhere. Its iron hand held both Anglicanism and Nonconformity in its grip. Exceptions like William Law were rare, and it needed no small courage to dissent from the generally accepted creed. But Wesley's heart and reason alike rebelled against the logical consequences of Predestination. Writing to his mother, he says, " How is this consistent with either the divine justice or mercy? Is it mercy to ordain a creature to everlasting misery? Is it just to punish crimes which he could not but commit? That God should be the author of sin and injustice—which must, I think, be the consequence of maintaining this opinion—is a contradiction of the clearest idea we have of the divine nature and perfections." And his mother agreed with him. " Predestination," she said, " was shocking, and ought to be abhorred."

But, if all may be saved, may they not *know* themselves saved? That was the problem which naturally presented itself to Wesley's acute mind. In another of those deeply interesting letters to his mother, which so clearly reveal the working of his mind at this period, he writes :

" If we dwell in Christ, and He in us (which He will not do unless we are regenerate), certainly we must be sensible of it."

Thirteen years were to roll by before the conviction was ratified by living experience, but it is significant that in this formative period we find the germ of the truth which was to eventually take a supreme place in the Methodist teaching.

But there was another great lesson to be learned,— Wesley's teachers, as we have seen, were narrow in their outlook. There was nothing in them to fore-shadow or suggest the great mission to the people. But God sometimes makes the humblest men messengers of His sublimest truths, and it was to a poor man in the Isle of Axholme that Wesley owed the seed-thought that afterwards brought forth so vast a harvest.

After obtaining his M.A. degree with great distinction, he returned home for a while to assist his father as curate; and it was during this time that one day he travelled several miles to talk with a "serious man," not far from the village where his father now held an additional living.

"Sir," said this nameless thinker, "you wish to serve God and go to heaven. Remember you cannot serve Him alone; you must therefore find companions or make them; **The Bible knows nothing of solitary religion.**"

The influences thus briefly outlined reached their height during the time that Wesley was Fellow of Lincoln. It was a strenuous life from every point of view. "Leisure and I have taken leave of one another," he wrote to his brother, Samuel. "I propose to be busy as long as I live, if my health is so long indulged me." But little did the men of Lincoln know what leaven was working among them. Lincoln College was founded in the fifteenth century by Fleming, the Bishop of Lincoln, who burned Wiclif's bones. Strange that it should be a Fellow of Lincoln who rekindled in England the fire that burned in Wiclif's soul.

In 1729 Wesley was recalled to Oxford, and for the first time appeared in the character of a "Methodist." During his first period at Oxford he was spiritually asleep. During the second he became thoroughly awake. But now he arouses himself to action. He becomes at once the recognised leader of the little group of men who are variously nicknamed Bible

Bigots, Bible Moths, The Holy Club, the Methodists.

John Wesley was not the first Oxford Methodist. That honour belongs to his brother Charles. Nor was the term altogether new. But though given in derision, it was transfigured by the character of the men who bore it. Wesley accepted it as a true description of what he and his fellows desired to be. " A Methodist," he said in later years, "is one that lives according to the *method* laid down in the Bible."

In the first instance the Holy Club consisted only of the two Wesleys, and two friends, William Morgan and Robert Kirkham. By degrees others joined, and the most notable addition was George Whitefield in 1735. The number, two years later, rose to twenty-seven.

It is unnecessary to give much space to the work of the Holy Club. Many of the men who formed it were associated with the Wesleys in later life, and did good work as clergymen of the Church of England.

At Oxford they were marked by the strictness of their lives, and by their many philanthropies. Wesley's religion was no longer entirely self-centred, but found vent in many activities. The one aim of these men was to *be* good and to *do* good. Some cultivated friendship with other undergraduates, with a view to helping them to more earnest Christian life. Some visited the poor of the city and taught them in their homes. Wesley himself founded a little school, and not only paid the mistress, but clothed the poorer children. Morgan set the example of visiting the prison, a work which involved real heroism. For gaol fever, a deadly form of typhus, was rife in the eighteenth century, and the Oxford prison was as insanitary as any. There was "no infirmary, no bath, no straw, and the prisoners lay in their clothes on mats. The felons' day room for *men* and *women*, down five steps, was twenty-three feet by eleven ; the men's dungeon, down five more, was eighteen by sixteen, with only small apertures, and swarming with vermin. The women's night room was seven feet by four." Debtors had to provide their own beds, and then pay eighteenpence a week for the privilege of lying on them. In fact, all the worst abuses of the day were in full force at Oxford, and the fellows and undergraduates who devoted themselves so nobly to the service of these poor and degraded prisoners were men of great soul and worthy purpose.

In 1735 Wesley's life at Oxford came to a close. The brave old man at Epworth closed a devoted life with a triumphant death. His last words were a prophecy, "Be steady. The Christian life will surely revive in this kingdom. You shall see it, though I shall not."

Of the Georgia missionary experience it is unnecessary here to write at length. Outwardly an apparent failure, it was actually a needful experience. It was Wesley's "Arabia," a desert episode from which he went forth to a world-wide mission vaster than had entered into the heart of any man of his time. The years spent in Georgia are well worthy of study, for in this over-sea colony Wesley gave his high views of Church order and discipline a full and fair trial, and the lessons were salutary. His character was tested in strange and unexpected ways, and when the story is fully told it will be seen that the intense humanness of the man was only exceeded by his noble spirit of loyalty to the divine voice. It was a period when many things hung in the balance, and at the end of it he sailed for England humbler and wiser, little dreaming that an event was at hand which would turn the current of a nation's history. In February 1738 he returned, and three months later the vast change took place which ushered in a Revival whose energies were to sweep round the globe.

VI.

THE THREE LEADERS

"*Great men exist that there may be yet greater men.*"—EMERSON.

74

THE THREE LEADERS

In the first chapter of this volume I have told the story of the epoch-making day when Wesley grasped, by thrilling personal experience, the truths which were to change the face of England and be felt to the utmost limit of the civilised world. Step by step we have studied the influences which went to the making of Wesley's character, and it has been shown how the varied spiritual energies of the past focussed themselves in his powerful personality. We have now to see how the new resultant force found expression in a movement which had for its aim the revival of scriptural Christianity,—a movement represented to-day, not only by the world-wide federation of Methodist churches, but also in the new life infused into almost every other branch of the Christian Church. But Wesley did not stand alone. By his side were others without whose aid the work could never have spread so swiftly, and it will be interesting to estimate the influence they exerted in the great campaign.

"Just at this time," says Wesley, "when we wanted little of filling up the measure of our iniquities, two or three clergymen of the Church of England began vehemently to call sinners to repentance. In two or three years they had sounded the alarm to the utmost borders of the land. Many thousands gathered together to hear them, and, in every place where they came, many began to show such a concern for religion as they had never done before" (*Works*, vol. vii. p. 203).

The three clergymen referred to were George Whitefield, Charles Wesley, and John Wesley—men at the best of their life, without benefice, without authority, and all three comparatively unknown. But they were men of great ideas. It was impossible to pen them up within the fence of a parish, or even within the shores of a sea-girt island. The world was in their hearts.

Whitefield was the **orator**, Charles Wesley the **singer**, and John Wesley the **statesman** of the movement. Equipped with varied and exceptional gifts, they stood shoulder to shoulder in the fight, but it is not a little remarkable that both Whitefield and Charles Wesley preceded John in the possession of that saving faith which became the keynote of their preaching.

Whitefield was of humble origin. He started life as tapster in a city inn. But there were latent powers which soon showed themselves when, as a humble servitor at Oxford, he entered the lists of university life. As with John Wesley, the reading of the *Imitation* and of Law's *Serious Call* made a profound impression upon his mind, and, after twelve month's residence at college, he became a member of the Holy Club.

When the Wesleys left for Georgia, Whitefield became the moving spirit among the Oxford Methodists. His struggles after the light remind one of the conflicts so graphically described by John Bunyan in *Grace Abounding.* For seven weeks he went through indescribable agony of soul, fasting, praying, hoping, despairing, and when at last he found deliverance, his " joys were like a springtide, and, as it were, overflowed the banks," and the happy experience once gained, deepened to the very end of life.

For such a man silence was impossible. The Word of God was a fire in his bones, and when it found expression, preaching became in his hands a new power. His first sermon was preached in St. Mary's, Gloucester, and it was reported to the fine old bishop who ordained him,—one of the best on the bench,— that fifteen of his hearers had gone clean mad. The bishop quietly remarked that he hoped the madness would continue.

His dramatic power as a preacher never rose higher than when preaching to the tens of thousands that crowded to Moorfields or Kennington Common to hear the great orator. The vast multitude of faces was like a wind-swept sea. Wave after wave of emotion spread from centre to circumference, smiles and tears rippled over the surface like sunshine and driven cloud. All sorts and conditions of men were there—great ladies, ecclesiastical dignitaries, street-hawkers and working-men, merchants and beggars of the slums, and all alike felt the power of his magnetic personality. He had no grace or beauty of person.

His eyes were small, and had a slight squint; his figure was stout, his dress careless, his wig often awry; but his voice was an instrument of magical sweetness and thrilling intensity. His eloquence swept off their feet the keenest intellects of the time. He appealed not to the head, but to the heart, and tears ran down the manliest face as he lifted up before his audience the crucified Saviour.

It was a refreshing change from the cold, devitalised moralities to which most congregations were accustomed. A hard-headed Scotchman put the matter in a nutshell when, reproved by his minister for listening to so irregular an evangelist, he replied, "Well, when I hear you I am planting trees all the time, but during the whole of Mr. Whitefield's sermon I had no time to plant even one."

Whitefield did not possess the fine gifts of statesmanship and theological acumen combined in John Wesley, and, when he separated from the Wesleys and became the leader of a distinct community of Methodists, the visible results of his work were comparatively small. But the influence of his oratory during the earlier years of the movement it is difficult to overestimate.

Charles Wesley was the **singer** of the new Pentecost, and his songs were even mightier than the eloquence of Whitefield. His individuality is to some extent overshadowed by the forceful personality of his greater brother, but no study of Methodist origins would be complete without an appreciation of the work done by Charles as well as John. Both were built in heroic mould, and in Charles Wesley we recognise the heroism of a man who rises above his strongest prejudices. He hated irregularity, and loved the liturgy, the rubrics, the decent and orderly worship of the Anglican Church; and for a man of his refined and delicate sensibility, with scholarly and even aristocratic tastes, to preach in the open, to fling aside the preferences of a lifetime, and to recognise the necessity of a hundred innovations, meant courage of no ordinary measure.

He also passed through the same spiritual conflict as his brother, and found the peace and assurance he desired just three days earlier. Curiously enough the Moravians were also instrumental in his enlightenment. Soon after his arrival in England, Peter Böhler " put himself under Charles Wesley's care to learn English," and through him the English clergyman learned the language of spiritual freedom. While acting as tutor to the Moravian, Charles Wesley had a serious illness. Böhler visited him, and spoke to him very faithfully. " For what reason do you hope to be saved?" he asked. " Because I have used my best endeavours to serve God," Charles replied. " Böhler," says Charles, in telling the story, " shook his head and said no more. I thought him very uncharitable, saying in my heart, 'Would he rob me of my endeavours? I have nothing else to trust to.' "

But the one who led him to the full knowledge of the Saviour was "a poor ignorant mechanic, who knows nothing but Christ." This was a brazier, called Bray; and the cultivated young clergyman insisted, ill as he was, on being carried to Bray's house, that he might learn from him the way of salvation. It was there that he read Luther *On the Galatians*, and the great forgotten truths of the Reformation became living in the heart and imagination of the Protestant clergyman of the eighteenth century.

With Charles Wesley's conversion a new note came into English song. The very first words that met his eye when he turned to the Bible on that eventful Whitsunday were, " He hath put a *new song* into my mouth." Charles Wesley was a poet, and he at once set himself to tell in musical and rhythmic phrase the story of his own deliverance. Within two days he had committed to writing the first stanzas of a hymn which more than any other expresses the spirit of early Methodism. Intense personal conviction and overflowing joy in God are linked with mighty appeal. The first stanza is full of the glow of his new and happy experience—

> " Where shall my wondering soul begin?
>   How shall I all to heaven aspire?
> A slave redeemed from death and sin,
>   A brand plucked from eternal fire,
> How shall I equal triumphs raise,
>   Or sing my great Deliverer's praise?"

But after a wonderful outpouring in verse after verse of love and devotion, the irresistible missionary and evangelistic impulse finds expression in the lines—

THE THREE LEADERS

" Come, O my guilty brethren, come,
      Groaning beneath your load of sin,
  His bleeding heart shall make you room,
      His open side shall take you in ;
  He calls you now, invites you home ;
      Come, O my guilty brethren, come ! "

It is little wonder, when songs like these went forth,
that the nation was moved to its very depths.

Charles Wesley's hymns are steeped in scriptural
thought. Some of them suggest the great ideas of
inspiration in every line. Nor are they merely a
beautiful mosaic of biblical phraseology : they illu-
minate Scripture. Many are intensely theological,
but the most abstract of sciences glows with vitality
when touched by Charles Wesley. No truth is too
deep, no thought too lofty, no conception too subtle
to elude the poet's grasp, and there are luminous,
expository, experimental hymns in which whole
sermons and treatises are crystallised into beautiful
and forceful expression.

One of the finest illustrations may be found in
another hymn belonging to the same period, the one
beginning with the lines—

      " And can it be that I should gain
          An interest in the Saviour's blood."

At least thirty-six passages of Scripture are *verbally*
and definitely illustrated. The third stanza is a
wonderful echo of Paul's great philosophy of the
" Kenosis "—the Emptying—in the second chapter
of the Philippians ; and it is scarcely possible to

F

THE THREE LEADERS

imagine anything finer than the parallel in the fourth stanza, between Peter's deliverance from prison and the emancipation of the soul—

> " Long my imprisoned spirit lay
>   Fast bound in sin and nature's night ;
> Thine eye diffused a quickening ray,
>   I woke, the dungeon flamed with light ;
> My chains fell off, my heart was free,
>   I rose, went forth, and followed Thee."

Charles Wesley's hymns have long overpassed all ecclesiastic boundaries, and have probably done more than any other influence to carry the energy and life of the evangelical revival into communions other than our own.

John Wesley was the **statesman** of the movement. He was a born general and organiser—a master of men.

His instincts as a leader come out grandly during the troublous early years of persecution.

Small in stature, with delicate, refined features, and quiet, gentle manner, he had an extraordinary power over the mob. He was a man of unquenchable courage. It was his principle "always to look a mob in the face." When riots broke out under the preaching of the Methodists in any part of the country, Wesley at once made his way to the centre of unrest to deal with the difficulty in person. The very light of his face seemed at times to still the tempest.

At Bolton, in 1742, a furious crowd, ready for any mischief, surrounded the house where he was.

A friend who went out to still them was seized, rolled in the mud, and pushed back into the house unrecognisable. Wesley quietly mounted a chair in the doorway, and looked round on the sea of angry faces. To use his own words, " The winds were hushed, and all were calm and still. My heart was filled with love, my eyes with tears, and my mouth with arguments."

At Plymouth the rabble was led by a young lieutenant and a number of riotous soldiers. Wesley waited a while, but finding that the passions of the crowd were becoming more and more inflamed, he stepped right out into the heart of it, took the captain by the hand, looking straight into his eyes. Instantly the man's whole demeanour changed. "Sir," he said, " I will see you safe home. Sir, no man shall touch you. Gentlemen, stand off, give back ! I will knock down the first man that touches him." And so the tall lieutenant and the little minister walked side by side till they reached the house where Wesley was staying, and then Wesley turned round and talked to the people, who eventually went away " in high good humour."

On another occasion, in Falmouth, the mob attacked the house where Wesley was. They were literally besieged, and the outworks were very soon carried, nothing but a thin partition separating them from the mob.

"Oh, sir, what shall we do ?" said Kitty, the daughter of the house.

"We must pray," said Wesley.

" But is it not better for you to hide yourself? "

"No," quietly replied the brave man. "It is best for me to stand just where I am."

By this time some reckless sailors, who evidently thoroughly enjoyed "parson baiting," put their shoulders to the door, shouting, "Avast, lads, avast!" and, at length, down it came with a crash. Without a moment's hesitation, Wesley stepped forward, walking right into the heart of the crowd as the crowd divided, saying, "Here I am. Which of you has anything to say to me? To which of you have I done any wrong? To you? Or you? Or you?" And then as the crowd hushed for a moment in sheer surprise, he cried, "Neighbours, countrymen! Do you desire to hear me speak?"

"Yes, yes," they shouted; "he shall speak," and the victory was won.

Another remarkable illustration may be found in the story of the well-known riot at Wednesbury, when, as Wesley began to pray aloud, the leader, a great hulking prize-fighter, put himself in front of Wesley and said, "Sir, I will spend my life for you! Follow me, and not one soul here shall touch a hair of your head."

When Charles Wesley, a few weeks later, asked "Honest Munchin," the ringleader in question "What think you of my brother?" he replied, "Think of him! That he is a mon of God: and God was on his side, when so mony of us could not kill one mon."

The same intrepid courage and genius for leadership are equally evidenced in later years, when it became necessary to tread unknown ways and to make bold experiments which only a great faith would ever have dared to attempt. A recent writer maintains that genius, so far from being associated with anything morbid or degenerate, is the uprush of an underlying personality greater than any of which we are conscious. In Wesley that may well have been true. Again and again we see him carried beyond himself, and in these moments of penetration and more than human insight we recognise not only a great spiritual genius, but also the touch of the divine hand.

These, then, were the Leaders, men of the age, each unique in his own line, but the greatest is John Wesley himself.

Charles had limitations from which his brother was free, but never were two brothers more loyal to one another. With John Wesley it was always, " My brother and I " ; and they worked lovingly together to the end. Charles Wesley himself said that the chief difference between them was that his brother's principle was, "First the Methodists, then the Church," while he reversed the order and would state it, " First the Church, then the Methodists." Theoretically, Charles held tenaciously to many of his early Anglican views, but in practice he was nearly as broad as his brother.

The differences between Wesley and Whitefield were more radical, and the divergence between the two men was evident in their preaching.

THE THREE LEADERS

Whitefield appealed to the emotions, Wesley was calm, judicial, logical; Whitefield thought in feelings, Wesley in syllogisms; Whitefield was swept along by the torrent of his own oratory, Wesley never lost self-control; the one awakened terrifying fears or ecstatic joys, the other carried home relentless conviction. Whitefield was like a storm that lashes the ocean surface into fury, Wesley was like the deep-sea current, never ceasing, never deflected; Whitefield saw in moments, Wesley had the vision of centuries; the present worth of Whitefield's sermons was perhaps the greater, but Wesley's had a capacity for accumulating power at compound interest.

With natures so different it is scarcely wonderful that they failed to see eye to eye on the great practical issues raised by the new order of things. For years they were estranged, though happily they were fully reconciled before Whitefield died. Whitefield, indeed, was in many respects a most lovable man; though Wesley, by his life work, added more to the sum-total of love in the world. In spite of all differences, Wesley recognised the true nobility of his early friend and co-worker.

A striking story, told in the *Contemporary Review* at the time of the Wesley Centenary, illustrates his humility and largeness of heart. Shortly after Whitefield's death, a lady who knew and reverenced both, and who was aware of their controversies, approached Wesley with some anxiety.

"'Dear Mr. Wesley, may I ask you a question?'

"'Yes, of course, madam, by all means.'

"'But, dear Mr. Wesley, I am very much afraid what the answer will be.'

"'Well, madam, let me hear your question, and then you will know my reply.'

"At last, after not a little hesitation, the inquirer tremblingly asked, 'Dear Mr. Wesley, do you expect to see dear Mr. Whitefield in heaven?'

"A lengthened pause followed, after which John Wesley replied with great seriousness, 'No, madam.'

"His inquirer at once explained, 'Ah, I was afraid you would say so.'

"To which John Wesley added, with intense earnestness, 'Do not misunderstand me, madam; George Whitefield was so bright a star in the firmament of God's glory, and will stand so near the throne, that one like me, who am less than the least, will never catch a glimpse of him.'"

John Wesley's character stands out the more grandly as we study it right through to the close of life.

He owed much to his magnificent constitution, to his strong common sense, and to his power of self-discipline.

He was a man of absolute honesty and unswerving truthfulness. He knew no fear; he was conspicuously free from jealousy and suspicion, and indeed from all the little meannesses of human nature.

He was a thinker of swift perception. In practical questions his decisions were quickly made and seldom revised; but when revision was necessary, it was frankly and boldly done.

Few men have been more open-minded. He welcomed the light, and showed his true greatness in his willingness to learn from the very humblest.

As a theologian he was governed by a strong love of reality and a keen historic sense. He possessed that quality of taste of which Ruskin says, that " it grasps all that it loves so hard that it crushes it if it be hollow."

His generalship has been already referred to. He was unquestionably commander-in-chief of his forces. But the power came to him unsought, and it was never exercised for selfish ends. It is not a little remarkable, that possessing almost despotic control, he everywhere won the hearts of his followers.

In scholarship, versatility, and in the saving sense of humour, he ranked high among the men of his day.

He was the busiest man in England. Few men have ever possessed such an enormous capacity for work. Dr. Johnson's one grumble at Wesley was summed up in the sentence, " He is never at leisure." During his strenuous life he travelled a quarter of a million miles, and preached no less than 40,000 sermons.

No man that has ever walked this earth, save One who was more than man, has been free from faults, and Wesley had his. He made mistakes, and he had one or two curious limitations. A lover of children he was singularly ignorant of child nature, as the extraordinary Spartan regulations for Kingswood School are evidence. He recognised, as few have done, the noble service that may be rendered by women to the Church of Christ; and yet women he never understood, and some of the greatest sorrows of his life are due to the fact.

Such was Wesley, and more: and this imperfect estimate of the man may help to the understanding of his work. It now remains to see how during Wesley's lifetime the foundations were laid, firm and strong, on which the whole superstructure of Methodism rests to-day.

VII.

THE GREAT METHO=
DIST YEAR: 1739 ·

" There is no other religious society under heaven which requires nothing of men, in order to their admission into it, but a desire to save their souls. . . . I do not know any other religious society, either ancient or modern, wherein such liberty of conscience is now allowed, or has been allowed, since the age of the Apostles."

WESLEY ("JOURNAL," 1788).

The beginnings of Methodism, — Chapels, Class Meetings, Evangelistic Work and Fellowship, all brought into existence during one wonderful year.

THE GREAT METHODIST
YEAR : 1739

THE year 1739 was a year of origins. It saw the first Methodist love-feast, the first field-preaching, the first dawn of the Class Meeting, and the building of the first Methodist chapel.

One of the most interesting gatherings of the early Christian Church was the *agape*, or love-feast. It was a simple, spontaneous expression of fellowship, and from it all forms of Christian worship have been little by little differentiated. The first believers met in singleness of heart, as those who belonged to one family. They broke bread together; they exhorted one another; they read at the homely meeting the letters from Paul or John that were handed from Church to Church; as time went on, after remembering the Saviour's dying love, they would read the names and recall the lives of brothers and sisters in Christ who had passed away. In earliest times it was the centre of the Church's life.

The Moravians revived this early institution, and Wesley borrowed the idea from them, admiring its simple and scriptural character; and on New Year's Day, 1739, the little group that instinctively clung to Wesley as their leader met for a love-feast in a room in Fetter Lane. It was not a Moravian meeting. It was the first *Methodist* Love-feast. Seven of those present were clergymen, and belonged to the Holy Club, but there were *sixty others*, the first-fruits of the great Church of the people so soon to be called into existence.

It was a memorable meeting, full of Pentecostal power. "About three in the morning," writes Wesley, "as we were continuing instant in prayer, the power of God came mightily upon us, insomuch that many cried out for exceeding joy. As soon as we were recovered a little from the awe and amazement at the presence of His Majesty, we broke out with one voice, 'We praise Thee, O God, we acknowledge Thee to be the Lord.'"

The love-feast became one of the most popular institutions of Methodism; but, in recent years, its form has become stereotyped, and its power is rarely that of the olden days.

The year thus begun was to carry the Methodist leaders far before it ended. In February, Whitefield went to Bristol, and experienced his first serious rebuff. The churches were closed to him. The only building where he obtained permission to preach was the gaol, the gaoler being one of his own converts, and there he spoke daily until that also was forbidden by order of the mayor and sheriffs.

Whitefield was not long in making his decision. Not far from Bristol was the colliery village of Kingswood, one of the new industrial populations springing up on the great coalfields, and practically ignored by the Church. The people were no better than heathen, notorious throughout the neighbourhood for their lawlessness and brutality. But to reach them he must preach in the open air, for they were absolutely without church or school, and on February 17th he spoke for the first time under the open roof of heaven. The congregation was only two hundred on this first occasion, but the numbers swiftly mounted up to two thousand and four thousand, and then to ten, fifteen, and twenty thousand. Day after day he addressed these closely packed multitudes. They stood on the walls, they clambered on waggons, they lifted each other into trees, and, as Whitefield pleaded, the tears made white channels down their grimy faces. No one had ever cared for their souls, and their hearts went out to the courageous preacher.

The work assumed such proportions that Wesley was invited by Whitefield to help him. But Wesley's instinct of order rebelled against the innovation. He writes—

" I could scarce reconcile myself at first to this strange way of preaching in the fields, having been all my life (till very lately) so tenacious of every point relating to decency and order, that I should have thought the saving of souls almost a sin if it had not been done in a church."

But on his arrival, he listened to Whitefield ; and in the evening, to stiffen his own resolution, he spoke to the little society, by this time formed, on the Sermon on the Mount, which was certainly an illustration of open-air preaching if ever there was one. The next day he flung prejudice to the winds, and preached to four thousand people from the text, "The Spirit of the Lord is upon me, because He hath anointed me to preach the gospel to the poor."

This was the first great breach in John Wesley's High Anglican defences. From this time forward he preached everywhere, and more often out-of-doors than in. On mountain and moorland, in Moorfields and Gwennap Pit, he illustrated the noble principle which he afterwards laid down for all his preachers, "Go, not only to those who want you, but to those who want you most."

But the most interesting event of the year was the *rise of the Class Meeting*. Strictly speaking, it did not take shape until later, but its roots go back to 1739.

The Class Meeting simply represents *the craving of earnest souls for fellowship and association.*

Methodism is an illustration of the fine old Cornish motto, "One and All." It believes in the power of the one, and in the still greater power which is gained by linking the ones into a unity. "There are some things of the religious life," says Phillips Brookes, "that a man can only learn in the company of his fellows." Wesley recognised the profound truth expressed in these words, and made fellowship the binding influence of the new movement.

Individuality is the centrifugal force of Christianity, and it needs to be balanced by the complementary force of association.

Every planet in the solar system has its own character, and, left to itself, would take its own course through the infinite fields of space. But, stronger than the impulse which would send it spinning aimlessly through wildernesses of death, is the silent influence which holds it in steady revolution round the sun, warmed by the sun's bright rays, and not alone, one of a group of planets similarly bound, similarly blest.

So when a man becomes a Christian, he does not lose his individuality, but he takes his place in a fellowship of souls, each one of which looks to Christ as the centre of his life. Fellowship is the centripetal force of the Church.

The first attempt to realise such a fellowship in something like a Class Meeting was at Bristol, not long after the events just described.

On April 4th, 1739, "in the evening three women agreed to meet together weekly, with the same intention as those in London, viz. 'To confess their faults one to another. . . .' At eight, four young men agreed to meet in pursuance of the same design." "How dare any man," asks Wesley, "deny this to be (in the substance of it) a means of grace ordained by God?"

The names of these Bristol Methodists deserve to be remembered.

It was a woman's idea. A Mrs. Panon "desired that she might propose the design to 'two others, Mrs. Norman and Mrs. Greville,' and offer them the liberty of joining." The four men were "Samuel Witham, a surgeon ; Richard Cross, upholsterer ; Charles Bonner, distiller ; and Thomas Westell, carpenter."

"If this work be not of God," says John Wesley, in the letter in which he gives these facts, "let it come to nought. If it be, who can hinder it?"

It was, in truth, the little Church crystallising into shape, following no lines of human organisation, but taking new forms of beauty designed by God Himself.

John Wesley gives a deeply interesting account of the origin of the Methodist Society in his *Appeal to Men of Reason and Religion*. He dates it from the fellowship meeting which became necessary in London the same year. Those whose lives had been changed through the preaching of the Wesleys, felt the need of guidance, encouragement, companionship, and Wesley advised them to meet together as often as possible.

"'But,' they said, 'we want you likewise to talk with us often, to direct and quicken us in our way, to give us the advices which you well know we need.'

". . . I asked, 'Which of you desire this? Let me know your names, and places of abode.'

"They did so. But I soon found they were too many for me to talk with severally so often as they wanted it. So I told them, 'If you will all of you come together every Thursday, in the evening, I will give you the best advice I can.'

"Thus arose, *without any previous design on either side, what was afterwards called a Society ;* a very innocent name, and very common in London for any number of people associating themselves together."

(*Works*, vol. viii. pp. 249, 250.)

The Class Meeting, as we now know it, took shape a little later in Bristol.

"The people were scattered so wide in all parts of the town, from Wapping to West=minster" (the boundaries east and west of continuous London a century and a half ago), "that I could not easily see what the behaviour of each person in his own neighbourhood was: so that several disorderly walkers did much hurt before I was apprised of it.

"At length, *while we were thinking of quite another thing, we struck upon a method for which we have cause to bless God ever since.* I was talking with several of the Society in Bristol concerning the means of paying the debts there, when one" (Charles Foy) "stood up and said, 'Let every member of the Society give a penny a week, till all are paid.' Another answered, 'But many of them are poor, and cannot afford to do it.' 'Then,' said he, 'put eleven of the poorest with me, and if they can give anything, well; I will call on them weekly, and if they can give nothing, I will give for them as well as for myself. And each of you call on eleven of your neigh=bours weekly; receive what they give, and make up what is wanting.' It was done. In a while some of these informed me, they

**found such and such an one did not live as
he ought.**

**" It struck me immediately, '*This is the
thing, the very thing, we have wanted so
long.***

**" As soon as possible, the same method was
used in London, and all other places."**

(*Works*, vol. viii. p. 252.)

In the story told by Wesley it is easy for us to
recognise the *instinct of association* working unconsciously among the people. But it was by no means
popular. The prejudices of the age were against it.
There is a curious illustration of this in the journal of
Thomas Twining, a clergyman of Wesley's day, and a
fair representative of the conventional ideas of the
time. He gives a lively description of the Gordon
riots in 1780, and then bursts into indignant protest :

" What punishment is too much for an endeavour to
inflame a people with religious animosity? especially
at such a time, when that kind of spirit has long been
quietly laid ; and mankind, if left to themselves, have
little or no propensity to that most horrible of vices
called zeal, . . . I am in hopes that good consequences may follow this convulsion, that it may be a
little help to open people's eyes, and to *bring into
disgrace the associating spirit*, by showing so evidently
its only tendency."

No doubt the " associating " Methodists would come
equally under his ban.

If it had not been for the Class Meeting, Methodism
would have been a rope of sand. Wherever the

Revival spread, there was the little meeting of Christians, a rallying point for all converts, in constant touch with the movement elsewhere, linking the units into a compact unity. And in these days, when the principle of association is illustrated in the powerful trusts, combines, and unions which, for good or ill, are revolutionising modern industry, there is need that, by every means in our power, we should strengthen the spirit of comradeship in the Church. But, unless we are to make the same mistake as the formalists of the eighteenth century, it must be kept in mind that the essential point is not the Class Meeting itself, but the principle of **fellowship** it is intended to express.

Before leaving the subject of fellowship, a word ought to be said as to Methodist **giving**. The financial bed-rock of Methodism is the "penny a week and a shilling a quarter," a method of systematic liberality the origin of which is told above. There are many wealthy, open-hearted laymen in our Church to-day who give largely of their abundance, but the whole fabric would crumble to pieces if we abandoned the regular weekly giving of the rank and file. The Methodist churches have always regarded giving as not merely a duty, but a privilege, a joyous element of religion, and not a mere irksome necessity. Their happiest and most prosperous members are the most generous. In the working out of the principle which has already so enriched us spiritually there is room for development, and probably nothing would do more to deepen and strengthen the best life of the

Church than a movement to promote consecrated, systematic, and proportionate giving.

The amazing rapidity with which events moved is shown by the fact that within a year of Wesley's great spiritual change the foundation was laid of the *first Methodist chapel*.

This was the "room" in Bristol, commenced on May 12th, 1739. Wesley appointed eleven trustees with himself, but they did very little to raise the necessary funds, and, on the suggestion of Whitefield, Wesley got rid of them, and took the entire responsibility upon his own shoulders.

He followed the same precedent in the case of nearly all chapels subsequently built, and the property of Methodism remained vested in himself until, by the Deed of Declaration, he transferred it to the Legal Conference.

The debts at Bristol referred to in the story of the Class Meeting were the debts on this little chapel, and it is interesting to note that they were paid out of the freewill offerings of the people. The Methodist "penny a week," envied by some notable students of the movement, originated in this first chapel-building scheme. Methodism has no tithes, endowments, or similar resources; the whole fabric rests on the love and generosity of its members and adherents.

A still more famous centre of spiritual influence was secured in London the same year. This was the old Foundery, not far away from the site of the present Book-room. For thirty-eight years it focussed the

activities of London Methodism, and was then super-
seded by City Road chapel.

Imagination lingers round the plain old building
where Methodism in the Metropolis first found a
home. It was little better than a ruin and was almost
entirely rebuilt, yet Wesley managed to get a chapel
seating fifteen hundred (part of it being used as a
schoolroom); a band-room holding three hundred, a
"book-room"; living rooms upstairs, used by Wesley
himself, and in which Susannah Wesley, his mother,
from this time lived and died; and, gradually, there
were added an almshouse and a dispensary, and it
became Wesley's base of operations for all kinds of
religious and philanthropic work.

So, swiftly and naturally the new movement took
shape. A review of the events of this wonderful year
makes one hesitate to speak of John Wesley as the
"founder" of Methodism. He was rather the inspired genius to whom it was given to recognise the
divine leading. The new departures of 1739 were
nearly all in the teeth of Wesley's most cherished
ideas. He never intended to take these critical steps.
He took them unwillingly. Some of the most fruitful
suggestions came from the people. The most remarkable fact about the events is their *spontaneity*.
As Wesley himself describes it, speaking of these
early Methodist workers :

**"As they had not the least expectation, at
first, of anything like what has since followed,
so they had no previous design or plan at all;
but everything arose just as the occasion**

offered. **They saw or felt some impending or pressing evil, or some good end necessary to be pursued. And *many times they fell unawares on the very thing* which secured the good or removed the evil."**

Particularly was this true of the formation of classes for fellowship under the guidance of leaders, the idea which has shaped organic Methodism. It suddenly flashed into the minds of Wesley and others while they "were thinking of quite another thing."

So the work grew, and, during this epoch-making year, were laid down clearly and firmly the lines which governed the whole of its after development. It will now be necessary to study the types of men created by the new order of things, the institutions that gradually took shape, and the teachings as to Church and faith which Methodism was destined to give to the whole world.

VIII.

JOHN WESLEY'S PREACHERS

"*Sacred Courage indicates that a man loves an idea better than all things in the world, and will venture all to put in act the invisible thought in his mind.*"—EMERSON.

Thomas Maxfield's daring innovation: Three representative preachers — Mitchell, Haime, and Nelson.

JOHN WESLEY'S PREACHERS

THE marvellous growth of Methodism, so powerfully illustrated by the events of one year described in the last chapter, made it impossible for any three men, however mighty in word and deed, to cover the work to be done, and there sprang into existence a *new order of preachers*, men of the people, and in some instances men of extraordinary power and heroic courage.

The first of these was Thomas Maxfield, one of the lay helpers, who, in the very earliest years of the Revival, attached themselves to Wesley and took charge of the new societies in his absence. While Wesley was on one of his journeys in 1742, Maxfield was left at the Foundery, where Susannah Wesley at this time had her rooms, and, carried away by his enthusiasm, he actually had the audacity to preach. Wesley soon heard of it and rode post haste to London. The idea of a layman preaching was contrary to all his ideas of ecclesiastical fitness. As he owned a few years later, he had "the deepest prejudices against it,"—"to touch this point was to touch the apple of my eye." So strong was his feeling that he determined at once to put a stop to the irregular proceeding.

But a conversation with his mother checked his impetuosity. His introduction of the subject was blunt enough.

"Thomas Maxfield has turned preacher, I hear."

"John," replied Mrs. Wesley, "you know what my sentiments have been. You cannot suspect me of favouring readily anything of this kind. But *take care what you do respecting that young man; for he is as surely called of God to preach as you are.*"

Wesley did the only sensible thing: he heard Maxfield preach, and was compelled to acknowledge the hand of God. From this day forward his scruples against lay preaching went to the winds, and, little by little, the new army of workers multiplied.

These men are worth studying if only for their heroism. "Methodism," said Isaac Taylor, was "expansive and adventurous," and the early preachers were true pioneers. An interesting comparison might be drawn between the sea-dogs of the Elizabethan time and the brave spirits of the Great Revival. England at the beginning of the sixteenth century was only an island with little outlook beyond itself, just as the religion of the eighteenth century was narrow and insular. And even as Queen Bess's sailors felt the call of the "great beyond," and with matchless daring steered their cockle-shells of boats into unknown seas, and along the coasts of new and fascinating lands, so the early Methodists conquered new worlds of experience, broke ground in untouched territories of the soul, and did so with a dauntlessness which loses nothing by comparison with the most fearless spirits of the dawntime of the Empire.

"If the hero be the sincere man, why should not every one of us be a hero?" said Carlyle. Certainly the early preachers were conspicuously sincere. Sincere, in the literal sense of the Greek equivalent, means "judged by the sun"; and the figure suggests the testing-room of a woollen mill, with its great windows from floor to ceiling, and its rolls of woven material unfolded yard by yard and scrutinised by practised eyes in the cold north light. There are plenty of lives that pass muster in the crowd, tested by the average standard of the day. But what are they like when judged by the sun?—by the glare of unfriendly criticism, by the cool north light of history, by the tests of Scripture?

By any of those standards these men are heroes,— true, honest, resolute, self-sacrificing,—men to admire, men to imitate.

The wealth of material for study is so great that it is difficult to make an adequate selection. Names crowd upon the memory: Thomas Walsh, the Irish saint, of whom Wesley said, "I love, honour, and admire him"; Olivers, the converted cobbler, to whom we owe one of the finest lyrics ever written; Christopher Hopper, the first itinerant in Scotland; Asbury, the pioneer of American Methodism. But these, and others, must be passed by in order to give larger space to three typical men, whose names are worthy to stand beside those of far greater fame.

The first of these is Thomas Mitchell, the "poor

man's preacher," as he was lovingly called, a man who possessed the heroism of a martyr. The story of his Lincolnshire persecution is one of the most touching in all the annals of Methodism.

It must be understood that Wesley's preachers were under his absolute command. They went where he bade them go, and they went on faith. They were at first absolutely dependent on the hospitality of the little societies that were springing up all over the land. At the very first Conference the principle was laid down—"Take no money of anyone. If they give you food when you are hungry, or clothes when you need them, it is good; but not silver and gold." Even Wesley himself was once reduced to a breakfast on blackberries. Not until 1752 was it decided that each itinerant preacher should have a stipend of £12 a year, to provide himself with necessaries.

It was a year earlier than this, on August 7th, that Mitchell arrived in the small hours of the morning in the little village of Wrangle, and by five o'clock he was preaching. But the room in which the service was held was soon stormed by an angry mob, led by two constables, who took the preacher into custody. For eleven hours, by order of the parish clergyman, the two officers of the law kept guard over him, and then handed him over to the rabble, who proceeded to duck him in a pool of standing water. The events which followed are best told in Mitchell's vivid and simple narrative.

" It took me up to the neck. Several times I strove to get out, but they pitched me in again. They told me I must go through it seven times. I did so, and then they let me come out. When I had got upon dry ground, a man stood ready with a pot full of white paint. He painted me all over from head to foot; and then they carried me into a public-house again. Here I was kept, till they had put five more of our friends into the water. Then they came and took me out again, and carried me to a great pond, which was railed in on every side, being two to twelve feet deep. Here, four men took me by the legs and arms, and swung me backward and forward. For a moment I felt the flesh shrink; but it was quickly gone. I gave myself up to the Lord, and was content His will should be done. They swung me two or three times, and then threw me as far as they could into the water. The fall and the water soon took away my senses, so that I felt nothing more. But some of them were not willing to have me drowned. So they watched till I came above water, and then, catching hold of my clothes with a long pole, made shift to drag me out."

Alarmed at their own handiwork, the ruffians dispersed, and Mitchell was carried, more dead than alive, into the house of a compassionate neighbour. But, hearing he was not drowned after all, the mob returned, dragged him out of bed into the street, and threatened to tear him limb from limb unless he pledged himself to preach there no more. But the plucky fellow plainly replied, "*I will promise no such thing.*"

Once again he got out of their clutches and was

put to bed; but in a little while his persecutors came back again, armed with fresh orders from the clergyman, and, though his clothes were unfit to put on, they put an old coat about him, hooted him out of the village, and, with a final jeer, "God save the King, and the devil take the preacher," left him to find shelter as best he might.

"Here," continues Thomas Mitchell, "they left me, penniless and friendless, for no one durst come near me. And my strength was nearly gone; so that I had much ado to walk. **But from the beginning to the end my mind was in perfect peace.** I found no anger or resentment, but could heartily pray for my persecutors."

It would scarcely be possible to find a nobler example of what Emerson calls "Sacred Courage," for certainly the brave Yorkshireman "ventured all to put in act" the consuming purpose that possessed him. "He endured as seeing Him who is invisible."

A man of a very different type was John Haime, the soldier-saint. He was simply a dragoon in the ranks, and fought in the last battle in which the British army was commanded by the monarch in person. His story is interesting, if only from the soldier's point of view, and doubly so when we realise the wonderful work he accomplished. Certainly the Christian life was no bed of roses to a British dragoon. Haime said he had three armies against him, "the French army, the wicked English army, and an army of devils." But this plucky soldier was by no means satisfied with fighting this triple foe on his own account; it was his great ambition to enlist his comrades in the same warfare.

His success was phenomenal. He was only a private in the ranks, with everything against him, and yet he built up a *society of three hundred Methodists*, six of whom became preachers like himself. So great was the respect he won from his superior officers that, when they went into winter quarters at Bruges, the General in command gave Haime permission to preach daily in the town church, and on Sunday the Methodist soldiers were marched to the service. Not infrequently he had as many as a thousand to hear him, and the officers and their families were attracted by the Methodist hymn-singing. During the week he would pay others to perform his camp duties while he tramped from camp to camp, preaching as often as five times a day, and for a week together.

And when it came to actual warfare, he was none the less courageous. At Dettingen he was in the thick of the fight. It was no long-distance conflict with an invisible enemy, as in modern times. The French troops were only separated from the British by the swift current of the Maine. Thousands were cut down by the musketry of the enemy, or by their still more murderous artillery. Haime's comrade on his left was struck down by his side. But fear he had none. In the hottest of the fray this brave Methodist soldier was communing with God in the sanctuary of his own heart. **"My heart was filled with love, peace, and joy, more than tongue can express. I was in a new world.** I could truly

say, ' Unto you that believe, He is precious.' I stood
the fire of the enemy seven hours."

One of the finest characters produced by Methodism was the *stalwart John Nelson*, a stone-mason by
trade, but a born thinker, and possessed of a ready
tongue, the sting of which was often felt by his
persecutors.

Nelson, longing for peace and forgiveness, went to
hear Wesley when he preached for the first time in
Moorfields. "As soon as he got up on the stand,"
says Nelson, "he stroked back his hair and turned
his face toward where I stood, and, I thought, fixed
his eyes upon me. His countenance struck an awful
dread on me, before I heard him speak, that it made
my heart beat like the pendulum of a clock, and
when he did speak, I thought his whole discourse was
aimed at me. When he had done, I said, ' This man
can tell the secrets of my heart ; he hath not left me
there, for he hath showed the remedy, even the blood
of Jesus.' "

At the time of his conversion he was working at
the Courts of Exchequer, Westminster, and very
courteously but firmly he refused to work on Sundays.
" The King's business requireth haste," argued the
foreman. But it was no use quoting Scripture to John
Nelson, who knew that "the devil himself can quote
Scripture on occasion." "Then religion has made
you a rebel against the King," he was told. " No,
sir," he made answer, "it has made me a better subject than ever I was. The greatest enemies the King
has are the Sabbath-breakers, swearers, drunkards,

whoremongers, for these pull down God's judgments upon King and country." Still the point was pressed. The Sunday work was made a condition of his retaining the place. "I will not wilfully offend God," he said, "for I had much rather want bread. It were better to beg bread barefoot to heaven, than ride in a coach to hell."

Nelson stuck to his guns, and when the Sunday was over, went back to fetch his tools. But, instead of dismissal, the foreman set him to work again, having evidently come to the conclusion that he would get more work out of the Methodist in six days than other men in seven. Nelson's reflection was, "I see it is good to obey God, and cast our care upon Him who will order all things well."

One of the most cruel and lawless attempts to silence him was in 1744, when troops were being raised to repel the invasion under the Young Pretender, an invasion which took place the following year. While preaching, he was seized by the constable, dragged before the commissioners, and forced into the army. Bail was refused, his friends were not allowed to open their lips in court, all evidence was suppressed, and the whole of the proceedings simply illustrate the truth of Nelson's own words at the time: "There is neither law nor justice for a man that is a Methodist." But in the sturdy Birstal mason they got more than they bargained for. He was a man of unconquerable spirit, and had an inconvenient knack of turning the tables upon his persecutors.

They flung him into Bradford town gaol, a horrible dungeon underneath the shambles, reeking with the blood and filth that soaked down into it. "But," says Nelson, "my soul was so filled with the love of God that it was a paradise to me."

Nelson's ready wit and marvellous knowledge of the Bible is illustrated by an incident that happened as the troops were passing through Boar Lane in Leeds. A "jolly, well-dressed" woman, who knew Nelson and had no great love for him, pushed her face close to his and said, "Now, Nelson, where is thy God? Thou saidst at Shent's door, as thou wast preaching, thou wast no more afraid of His promise failing than thou wast of dropping through the heart of the earth." Instantly Nelson replied, "Look in the seventh chapter of Micah, and the eighth and tenth verses." The verses are these—

"Rejoice not against me, O my enemy: when I fall, I shall arise; when I sit in darkness, the Lord shall be a light unto me."

"Then she that is mine enemy shall see it, and shame shall cover her that said unto me, Where is the Lord thy God?"

To the woman herself, if she was curious enough to look for them, the words must have seemed nothing less than a direct message from God Himself.

In York he was brought before the officers of the regiment he was intended to join; but stirred by their godless language, the man who had been dragged into the army to prevent his preaching, delivered his testimony against profanity in no measured terms.

"You must not preach to your officers," said one of them, as soon as he could get his breath.

"There is but one way to prevent me," said Nelson.

"What is that?" they said.

"To swear no more in my hearing," replied the new recruit.

It was awkward for the military authorities that Nelson would not take the King's money. They tried the effect of a night in prison with a plank bed, but the prisoner slept as if he "had been on a bed of down." Then they court-martialled him, and the Methodist preacher was guarded to his judges by a file of musketeers with bayonets fixed. In two minutes he was preaching again, and seeing that he roundly affirmed that he would not fight, they had to be satisfied with his assurance that he certainly would not run away.

For three months they tried to turn the preacher into a soldier, but they found in Nelson a stronger will than their own. He never complained, never disobeyed orders, and never forgot his consuming passion for souls. He always got the last word, and it was a word that searched the heart. The only result of his compulsory service was the spread of Methodism, not only throughout his regiment, but wherever his regiment went; and when his release was ordered, his major said, "I wish I had a regiment of such men as he is in all respects, save that one, his refusing to fight: I would not care what enemy I had to meet."

There were times when Nelson seemed to be

literally an inspired man. His power over a mob had something almost supernatural about it. "His look is not like that of other men," would be said sometimes.

One of his most remarkable escapes was at Horbury, near Wakefield. The roughs of the neighbourhood determined to put an end to him. This "Methodist dog" should be drowned as he deserved, with a halter round his neck. The attack was organised by the "parson's son," and their plans were laid with some knowledge of the man with whom they had to deal. Six hand-bells were jangled to drown his voice, the biggest men in the town—a butcher and a half-crazy fellow six feet high—were put in charge of the halter ; and thus prepared, they surrounded the house where Nelson was at breakfast. But when he came out to face them, their diabolical plans all went awry. Nelson simply raised his hand to push away the halter, and the big fellow who held it fell to the ground "as if felled with an axe." The butcher stood trembling and unable to move. When the constable, as usual on the side of the mob, came forward to take Nelson into custody, "I am glad you are come," said Nelson, "and I charge you in the King's name to do your office." "What is my office ?" the constable replied. "To quell this mob," said Nelson, "and deliver me out of their hands. If I have broken the law, take me to a magistrate to be punished by the law." The man turned pale, bid the mob be quiet, forced a way through to the stable where Nelson's horse was, saddled it, held his stirrup for him, and saw him safely out of town.

There were occasions, it is true, when Nelson was overpowered by the brutality of his persecutors; and when we read what he went through, how he was left for dead, and, bleeding, bruised, and helpless, was again dragged by the hair over the rough cobble stones of the village street, we do not wonder that his enemies said, "I have heard that a cat has nine lives; but I think he has nine score."

These, and others like them, were the men who made Methodism, confessors of which any Church would have a right to be proud, and the remembrance of their steadfastness and devotion ought to kindle anew the fire of enthusiasm in the men of our own time. The moral of their lives is summed up in the stirring words on the Methodist Revival uttered by President Roosevelt.

"If we are to advance in broad humanity, in kindliness, in the spirit of brotherhood, exactly as we advance in our conquest over the hidden forces of nature, it must be by developing strength in virtue, and virtue in strength, by breeding and training men who shall be both good and strong, both gentle and valiant,—men who scorn wrong-doing, and who, at the same time, have both the courage and the strength to strive mightily for the right."

IX.

THE STORY OF THE CONFERENCE

*" The help of good counsel is that
which setteth business straight."*
            BACON, ESSAY XXVII.

*" That is the happiest conversation
where there is no competition, no
vanity, but only a calm, quiet interchange of sentiment."— DR. JOHNSON.*

*A manuscript copy of
the earliest Minutes.
Famous   Conferences.
The Conference of to-
day.*

THE STORY OF THE CONFERENCE

In the Headingley College library there is a little volume, bound in paper boards, six inches by four, entitled, " *Minutes of some late Conversations between the Rev. Mr. Wesley and Others.*" It is not printed, but written by hand, and some of the corrections are in Wesley's own writing. The little book belonged to Wesley himself, and was carried by him in his pocket or in his saddle-bags as he journeyed all over England. It is a manuscript copy of the *first* "Minutes of Conference."

" *The Minutes*,"—every Methodist knows them to-day, black volumes, gold lettered, getting stouter and stouter every year, and packed with information from cover to cover.

We have travelled far since Wesley's day, and yet the very title-page of the latest volume links us with the first Conference in 1744.

It is headed "Wesleyan Methodist *Church*"— which certainly does not appear in the little manuscript volume. The Church, then, was only in germ.

But underneath we read, "Minutes of several Conversations at the one hundred and fifty-ninth Yearly Conference of the People called Methodists, in the connexion established by the late Rev. John Wesley, M.A., begun in Manchester, on Tuesday, July 22, 1902."

Half-way through the book, which contains no less than 696 pages, after a loyal address to His Majesty the King, we find an address to the "Methodist Societies," addresses to or replies to addresses from the Irish, French, South African, West Indian, and Canadian Conferences. And a visitor to the Conference itself would find that these are not all, for on the Conference platform there are men representing great Conferences in the United States and in far Australia.

What is the "Conference," and how did it begin?

As the "Minutes" were not printed year by year until 1749, these precious little volumes are of special and peculiar interest.

In 1744, then, six years after the Wesleys and Whitefield began their marvellous campaign, the first Conference was held in London. Wesley was a man who had "understanding of the times." His statesmanlike mind foresaw that if the work was to endure, it must be strengthened by careful organisation.

As we have seen, the Class Meeting was already in existence. There were two thousand members in London alone. The preachers numbered forty-five, and there were preaching places not a few. Some of the preachers were clergymen, helping as they were able. But most were laymen, working for their living, and, as they could afford to do so, making their preaching tours far and near, as Wesley directed them. It was high time for *Conference*, for conversation as to the "next step," and Wesley did wisely to take his workers into council with himself on the pressing questions of the hour.

The Conference met at the Foundery, and was entertained during its sessions by the Countess of Huntingdon. This lady was one of a group of noble women who played no small part in the early days of Methodism. She was among the earliest to recognise the power of the Wesleys, and not only became a Methodist herself, but used her influence among the men and women in high life among whom she moved. Even in the bad old days of George II., her character was a leaven for good. One day, so it is said, the Prince of Wales asked why Lady Huntingdon absented herself from Court circles. A flippant lady replied, "I suppose she is praying with her beggars." The prince looked grave and replied, "Lady Charlotte, when I am dying, I think I shall be happy to seize the skirt of Lady Huntingdon's mantle to lift me up to heaven." Such an incident speaks volumes as to the esteem in which she was held by the very highest in the land. As is well known, she inclined, with Whitefield, to Calvinism, and founded a "Connexion," known as Lady Huntingdon's Connexion. But to the end of her life she maintained a warm friendship with the Wesleys.

In her aristocratic mansion, then, and in the plain old Foundery, met the men who were shaping the new movement; and we turn again to the little brown volume to see if we can find any resemblance between this little gathering and the great representative assembly of to-day.

At the outset we note that it was a Conference of **ministers and laymen,** or, more strictly speaking, of clergymen and itinerant lay-preachers, for none of Wesley's assistants were as yet formally ordained. But a year later, at Bristol, a layman, Marmaduke Gwynne, who never became a preacher, was present, and in him we find the prototype of those loyal and devoted men who, generation after generation, have given noble service to the Methodist Church.

The names of those who were present at the first Conference must not be forgotten. In addition to John and Charles Wesley, there were John Hodges, a Welsh rector; Henry Piers, vicar of Bexley; Samuel Taylor, vicar of Quinton; and John Meriton, a clergyman from the Isle of Man, who journeyed extensively in the endeavour to spread the influence of Methodism. There were also four lay-preachers—Thomas Maxfield, Thomas Richards, John Bennet, and John Downes.

All the business was done by the method of question and answer; and if we turn to the very latest volume of the "Minutes of Conference," we shall see at a glance that this common-sense way of securing that subjects of perennial importance shall be regularly attended to, is still maintained.

No one can fail to recognise the earnestness and open-mindedness of John Wesley and his friends. At their very first meeting they laid down principles for their mutual guidance which one cannot but admire.

"It is desired that all things be considered as in the immediate presence of God; that we meet with a single eye, and as little children who have everything to learn; that every point be examined from the foundation; that every person may speak freely whatever is in his heart; and that every question proposed may be fully debated and bolted to the bran."

As a matter of fact, we do find a very frank and courageous discussion of many points which were then by no means the commonplaces of to-day.

The subjects of conversation centred round three practical questions, viz.

1. What to teach;
2. How to teach; and
3. What to do.

The first two days were spent in the discussion of Doctrine, and it was only on the third day that they came to matters of Discipline and Church Order; and, under the last-named point, it is interesting to see how Wesley foresaw that it might become impossible for his followers to remain in the Church of England.

"We are persuaded that the body of our hearers will even after our death remain in the Church, *unless they be thrust out.* We believe, notwithstanding, either that they will be thrust out, or that they will leaven the whole Church."

It became more and more evident as time went on that the Church was unwilling to be leavened, and

Wesley made full provision for the other and less welcome alternative.

In this very first Conference we find many of the terms familiar in modern Methodism, with a few that have gone out of use. We read of ministers—then used of the clergy only; assistants—a term used to describe preachers in charge of a group of societies; stewards; leaders; visitors of the sick; and schoolmasters; and their duties are carefully defined. We have everything in germ which is characteristic of Methodism as distinct from other ecclesiastical organisations.

The Rules of an assistant, still read every year at Conference, Synod, and Preachers' Meeting, are here, with merely verbal differences, striking, in the very first words, the keynote of thoroughness and industry.

" Be diligent, never be unemployed a moment, never be triflingly employed."

And from that day to this no Methodist preacher, loyal to these first principles, has had time to be other than a busy man.

From 1744 onwards the Conference met regularly once a year. It was summoned by Wesley himself, and consisted of those whom he invited to join him in consultation. Little by little it grew, and it will be interesting to note a few of the more notable Conferences which stand out as landmarks in the history of Methodism.

1747. In 1747, at the next Conference held in London, Wesley and his preachers arrived at some very remarkable conclusions with regard to *Scriptural Church Organisation*. For this we must turn to what are called the "Bennet Minutes," another little manuscript volume which belonged to John Bennet.

Take the following questions and answers by way of sample.

Q. **What instance or ground is there in the New Testament for a national church?**

A. **We know none at all. We apprehend it to be a mere political institution.**

Q. **Are the three orders of Bishops, Priests, and Deacons plainly described in the New Testament?**

A. **We think they are, and believe they generally obtained in the churches of the apostolic age.**

Q. **But are you assured God designed the same plan should obtain in all churches throughout all ages?**

A. **We are not assured of this, because|we do not know that it is asserted in Holy Writ.**

Q. **In what age was the divine right of episcopacy first asserted in England?**

A. **About the middle of Queen Elizabeth's reign. Till then all the Bishops and Clergy in England continually allowed and joined in the ministrations of those who were not epis= copally ordained.**

Q. **Was there any thought of uniformity in the government of all churches until the|time of Constantine?**

THE STORY OF

A. It is certain there was not; and would not have been then, had men consulted the Word of God only.

It is clear from these statements that Wesley's idea as to Episcopacy and Church government were undergoing a radical change.

1769.

The Leeds Conference of 1769 will ever be memorable as the one which sent out the *first preachers to* America. When Wesley asked, "Who is willing to go?" and Richard Boardman and Joseph Pilmoor responded, no one dreamed of the wonderful work to be done in the New World. The Methodist Episcopal churches of the United States are to-day the wealthiest Protestant churches in the world, and it is strange to look back to that little gathering of preachers in the West Riding of Yorkshire, and to note the question and answer that follow the appointment of the two pioneers.

"What can we do further in token of our brotherly love?"

"Let us now make a collection among ourselves."

And these poor but generous men at once contributed £70, of which £20 was to pay the passage of the two preachers, and the remainder to be carried by them as a gift of love towards the building of the first Methodist church beyond the Atlantic.

1784.

Another Leeds Conference held fifteen years later, in 1784, may be described as epoch-making. It was

130

the Conference at which the famous *Deed of Declaration* was accepted,—the "Magna Charta of British Methodism," as an American writer has described it. This was the document by which Wesley, now an old man, handed over his unique and almost autocratic power to a hundred of his preachers nominated by himself.

John Wesley's "Deed of Declaration," sometimes briefly called the "Deed Poll," was a step of the first importance. It gave Methodism a recognised status, it provided for continuity of government, and prepared the way for the separate existence of Methodism as a Church, if "thrust out" by the Establishment.

The chief powers assigned to the Conference, or to the Legal Hundred as composing the *Legal* Conference, are those of filling up their own ranks year by year, electing the president, appointing the preachers, deciding who shall be and who shall not be preachers, and the holding of Methodist Church property. The Deed Poll is responsible for the itinerancy. No preacher may be appointed to any chapel for more than three years in succession, except in the case of "ordained ministers of the Church of England." It is interesting to note that, besides the Wesleys, there were several clergymen members of the Conference, who laboured as Methodist preachers in Circuits to the end of their lives. One of these was James Creighton, an Irish clergyman, who preached in barns, old ruins, anywhere and everywhere so long as he got a congregation. "I never saw any fruits of my labour until I became irregular," he said.

Wesley accepted him as one of his assistants, and he worked chiefly in London. So also with others, but in accordance with the Deed of Declaration, they were not compelled to "move on" at the end of three years. The "itinerancy" has proved itself to be a wise and healthy principle, but even Wesley recognised that there might be exceptions.

Between thirty and forty years ago, when an Act of Parliament was sought to give similar powers to Conferences in Canada, Australasia, and South Africa, the Deed Poll was carried down for examination to the House of Lords. The peers present, including some of the great Law Lords, clustered round the table to look at the curious old document signed by John Wesley himself, and one and all expressed amazement at the skill and sagacity evidenced in the drawing up of this brief but far-reaching instrument. It undoubtedly ranks as one of the most interesting legal documents in the world.

1791. On Wednesday, March 2nd, 1791, John Wesley died, and the Conference that met in Manchester the following July had to face the future.

More than three hundred preachers were present, the largest number ever convened together. The last message of the great leader to his fellow-workers, contained in a sealed letter written six years before, was read to the Conference. It contained one very significant sentence. The Conference was advised to carry on the work on the same lines as during Wesley's life, *"so far as circumstances will permit."*

It was at once determined that all the preachers in full connection with the Conference should share in its privileges and administration so far as the Deed of Declaration would allow, the Hundred reserving to themselves only the final vote.

But there were questions of pressing importance which, during the next few years, had to be fairly considered and settled. There were three distinct classes of Methodists. Some inclined to the Anglican Church, others to Dissent, and a still greater number steered a middle course between the two. The burning question was, "Shall all the preachers administer the Sacraments." The Church party said, "No"; the advanced party said, "Yes, and at once"; the majority advised patience and consideration.

1792. At the London Conference it became evident that the voice of the people was for independence, for that was what the step meant. It could hardly be called *separation* from the Church, for the vast majority of Methodists had never been in the Church, and therefore could not come out of it. As an acute Yorkshireman put it, "If we are not *Dis*senters, we are *ab*senters." But the feeling ran so high that eventually the Conference drew lots, and the result was postponement for another year.

1793. Once again a critical question came up for discussion at Leeds; and in 1793, without any bitterness, it was agreed that, wherever a Society was unanimous, the preachers should have power to administer the Sacraments.

1794. At the next Conference there was trouble with the trustees. In several places they claimed the power to veto the decision of the previous year. It was an important point. The unity of Methodism depended upon the decision, and it was made clear that the Conference must be supreme.

1795. It was not until a year later, at Manchester, that the problem was finally solved by a measure called "*The Plan of Pacification.*" This provided that the Sacraments should be administered wherever a *majority* of the trustees, and of the stewards and leaders were in favour, but that such decision, once given, was not to be revoked.

This step was decisive. It marked the fact that Methodism was practically outside the Church of England. It was simply a logical recognition of events. This statesman-like measure made clear three points.

1. That, under the circumstances named, the preachers had permission to administer the Sacraments.
2. That the Conference had sole power to appoint preachers.
3. That the trustees were responsible for seeing to the fitness of preachers so appointed.

It has been necessary to give these successive stages in detail, as these five years were the most critical of the early years of Methodism. The decision arrived at did not, of course, satisfy all. On the one hand there were the Church Methodists, who were reabsorbed into the Church, or, some years later, formed themselves into a separate community, going to the parish church for the Sacraments, and acknowledging in other ways the authority of the Establishment. And at the opposite pole there were the extremists, who were hostile to the Church, and who joined one or other of the off-shoots of Methodism more in harmony with their own views.

Of the divisions of Methodism it is not necessary to tell the story. Some were in order to secure reforms which would have come with years. Some were due to misunderstanding. To-day it is doubtful whether there is any really vital point of difference between the various branches of the Methodist family. In Ireland, Canada, and Australasia, complete reunion has been happily accomplished, and, whatever may be the slight differences of administration, *Methodism is to-day absolutely one in doctrine*. Save for a very insignificant secession in 1835, there never has been any division on questions of faith, and the great truths which moved England and America in the eighteenth century are as clearly preached to-day as in the days of the Wesleys.

1877. Perhaps the greatest change in the Conference during the last century was the adoption of *Lay Representation* in 1877. As early as 1801, laymen began to attend the Synods, or District Meetings, as they were then called ; and for many years, in the old Committees of Review, laymen met in council with the ministers. But the new legislation gave laymen a definite place in the

Conference itself, and it is to-day generally agreed that the Conference has gained immeasurably in influence. As one or two changes have since taken place, it may be well to close this chapter with an outline of the Order of Conference as now in force.

The Representative Session of the Conference now meets first, and consists of three hundred ministers and three hundred laymen. The president and secretary are nominated the previous year by the Pastoral Session, and the first business, after filling up any vacancies in the Legal Hundred caused by death, is their election by the Legal Conference. The representatives are chosen by the May Synod, and the laymen must be members of the Church of at least five years' standing, and be already trustees, members of some Quarterly Meeting, or of the Synod, —in brief, they must be *workers*, definitely rendering some kind of service to the Church.

The business of the Representative Session is largely financial, and deals with the administration of the great departments of Methodism, including Foreign Missions, Home Missions, the Theological Colleges, Education, Sunday Schools, the Wesley Guild, Temperance, and similar questions.

In this, as in the Pastoral Session, the conversation on the work of God always holds a prominent place.

The Pastoral Session deals mainly with doctrine, discipline, the reception of candidates, and appointment of ministers. Probably no Church in the world goes so thoroughly into matters of doctrine, character, and fitness for the work, as our own.

The Ordination Service is a session of the Pastoral Conference, and nothing could be more impressive. Ordination is by laying on of hands, a practice adopted in 1836, as in harmony with primitive usage. The president with two or three other senior ministers lay hands on each candidate, and a charge is delivered by the retiring president.

Such, in barest outline, is the story of the Methodist Conference, and, whether we speak of the mother Church, or of the many Conferences which have sprung from it, it is in all cases an assembly of *real administrative power*.

Convocation in the Anglican Church is strictly limited in its range of influence. It has no power in the parish. It appoints no clergyman, and no vicar or curate can by its authority be called to account. The Assemblies of the Scotch Churches have legislative power, but much more restricted in range. The Congregational and Baptist Unions are purely voluntary and deliberative. But the decisions of the Methodist Conferences are frankly and cheerfully accepted by Methodists everywhere, and for the reason that the Conference represents the ministers and people of Methodism all over the world.

Before passing from the subject of the Conference, a few words should be added with regard to the *District Synods*, which were, in the first instance, simply committees of the Conference.

The actual division of the whole country into districts first took place in 1791, the year of John Wesley's death. There was no arrangement for an annual meeting. The preachers were simply called together at any time by any superintendent minister who wished to have the advice of his brethren.

In 1797 the Chairmen of Districts were elected by ballot of the Conference, and shortly afterwards the District Committee became a stated annual assembly. Its name was changed to *Synod* in 1892.

It does not fall within the scope of this work to outline the business. The *Order and Form of Business*, containing not only the subjects dealt with, but also a digest of the laws and regulations under each head, is itself a volume of more than a hundred pages, and reference may be made to it by those who want fuller information.

To-day the Synod is not merely ministerial. On the second day of the annual meetings in May, and at the September Synod, laymen are present, including district lay officers, circuit stewards or their substitutes, and representatives elected by each Quarterly Meeting. The presence of this large lay element, changing to a great extent from year to year, immensely increases the interest of the circuits in district administration, and tends to promote a spirit of unity and progress.

The District Synod in its Pastoral Session is one of our Methodist Courts of Discipline, and a Court of Appeal for members who have been found guilty under any charge before the Leaders' Meeting.

THE CONFERENCE

It may perhaps be useful here to sketch in bare skeleton the scheme of Methodist discipline. A different course is taken with regard to ministers, local preachers, trustees, leaders, and members.

Regular inquiry is made at the May Synod with regard to the character, orthodoxy, loyalty, and ability of each individual minister. No name, in any circumstances, is passed over. If a charge be preferred against any minister during the year, it is heard before a minor Synod, and the report presented to the May Synod, and handed on to Conference.

Leaders or members who are accused are tried by the Leaders' Meeting, and if found guilty they have right of appeal to a minor Synod, the Annual District Synod, and the Conference.

A trustee against whom any charge is brought, must be tried before a court composed of his fellow-trustees and the Leaders' Meeting of the same Society.

A local preacher is answerable, in all matters that concern *his standing as a local preacher*, to the Local Preachers' Meeting, but as a member he is amenable with all others to the Leaders' Meeting.

There are other special courts, but these are the most important. The essential point is to note that purity of life and doctrine are guarded at every point. There is no expensive legal system. There are no ecclesiastical lawyers. Discipline is maintained by the simplest means and at the lowest cost, and the very poorest member is assured of his rights as a member of the Christian Church without any cost to himself.

X.

THE METHODIST PARISH AND ITS COUNCILS

" *There are to be no useless hands or sleeping partners in the Church's business, none who receives without giving back. In a healthy body every tissue, fibre, and artery has its office to discharge, nothing is wasted or inert or superfluous; so in a healthy Church, 'According to the effectual working in the measure of each single part, it builds up itself in love.' Such was St. Paul's ideal for the Societies he founded; it is the ideal of Methodism.*"—G. G. FINDLAY, B.A., D.D.

The Circuit. Its central gathering, and its smaller councils for spiritual, financial, and evangelistic purposes.

THE METHODIST PARISH AND ITS COUNCILS

In very old days, before the Norman Conquest, England was divided into townships, and the townships were grouped into hundreds. The township, in Anglo-Saxon times, was the unit of local government.

Then came Christianity, and the land was mapped out in parishes for purposes of ecclesiastical convenience, and until Methodism arose, the parish was the only religious unit, which included in the aggregate the whole country. Travel where you will, you are never out of a parish. The institution of the civil parish was of later date, and was really a revival of the old Saxon township under a different name.

The *Circuit* is the Methodist parish. A Methodist Atlas—and there is or was such a thing—takes in every acre of Great Britain and Ireland. Snowdon, Helvellyn, Dartmoor, Epping Forest—no corner is left out. The loneliest shepherd's hut among the hills of Wales or Scotland is in some circuit or other, and all the chapels and preaching places within the area of a given circuit are linked together under one common government.

John Wesley had the instincts of a great commander. In a very few years he saw that the work he

and his preachers had to do was only to be bounded by
the Seven Seas, and with military thoroughness he proceeded to map out the country. As early as 1746 England and Wales were divided into *seven* circuits. To-day,
including the foreign field, there are over a thousand,
and as the Church grows they will continue to multiply.

The circuit, like every other part of our organisation, has had a gradual development. And just as in
the Northrop loom, with its electric motor, its delicate
adjustments, its lightning speed, and its shuttle changing automatically when the thread is spent, you can
still see the old hand-loom of a hundred years ago ;
so in the compact modern circuit, with its up-to-date
methods and economy of power, you can see a distinct relationship to the simple arrangements necessi-
tated by the spread of Methodism in the middle years
of the eighteenth century.

As already pointed out, circuits are first mentioned
in the manuscript Minutes of 1746. But in two years
they had become so numerous as to be grouped into
nine districts, each including a number of circuits
within its borders.

To each circuit an *assistant* was appointed, with
one or more *helpers*. These were the itinerant
ministry of the day, and they were under the personal direction of Wesley himself.

Their duties are outlined by Wesley in *Works*,
vol. viii. p. 319, and include some of the most important responsibilities of modern circuit life. They
were—

" (1) To see that the other preachers in his

circuit behave well, and want nothing. (2) To visit the Classes quarterly . . . and deliver Tickets. (3) To take in or put out of the Society, etc. (4) To keep Watchnights and Love=feasts. (5) To hold *Quarterly Meetings*, and therein diligently to inquire into both the temporal and spiritual state of each Society. (6) To take care that '*every Society be duly supplied with books.*'" On this Wesley says emphatically: "The Societies are not half sup= plied with books . . . Oh! exert yourselves in this. Be not weary. Leave no stone un= turned." "(7) To send from every Quarterly Meeting a circumstantial account to London of every remarkable conversion and remark= able death. (8) To take exact Lists of his Societies every Quarter, and send them up to London. (9) . . . To overlook the Accounts of all the Stewards."

(*Works*, vol. viii. p. 319.)

The Methodist parish has its *Councils*, and chief among these is the Quarterly Meeting.

We first read of the Quarterly Meeting in 1750, when John Bennet, one of the preachers, was asked to draw up a plan for its conduct. But its constitu= tion was not fully defined until 1852, more than a hundred years later.

A stranger entering a Quarterly Meeting would at once be impressed by its popular character. Method= ism is in the best sense a Church of the people, and the fact is very evident in this administrative assembly.

In a large circuit there will be from one to two hundred entitled to attend. County magistrates, lawyers, aldermen, blacksmiths, carters, coachmen, manufacturers, tradesmen,—all sorts and conditions of men are there, and all are interested. By no process of direct election would it be possible to get a more representative gathering.

It is a **council of *workers*.** Everyone is present in virtue of some duty assigned, or of some service actually rendered.

First of all there are the *ministers* appointed by Conference, the superintendent at their head. He is a " bishop," in the New Testament sense of the word, and his official designation is simply a literal Latin translation of the Greek " episkopos," and signifies an " overseer." Supernumerary ministers resident in the circuit have also the right to be present.

Foremost among the circuit officials are the *circuit stewards*. They are the financiers of the meeting, responsible for the circuit income, receiving the monies from the society stewards and reporting to the meeting the income and expenditure. They pay all allowances and connexional assessments, and look after the furnishing and renewal of the ministers' houses. In a Church where the term of residence is only three years, some such arrangement is necessary, and it is difficult to estimate the service so willingly rendered by earnest and large-hearted laymen. Ex-stewards have also seats in the meeting, and their experience is often of value to their successors.

A third group consists of the *society stewards, poor*

stewards, and *class leaders* of the various societies. In a circuit where there are ten or twelve chapels, there will sometimes be seventy or eighty such workers, men and women, directly interested in the most spiritual service of the Church.

Another field of work is represented by the *local preachers*, all of whom, if fully accredited, have the right to be present.

Property interests are under the care of the *trustees*, and every trustee of every chapel in the circuit has a seat, provided that he is a member of some society within the circuit.

Sunday schools are entitled to send the *senior superintendent* and one or more representatives, according to the size of the school. In all cases such representatives must be church members of three years' standing.

The **business** is essentially practical.

After the reading of the Minutes follows the quarterly budget, presented by the circuit stewards, a careful and detailed statement of receipts and expenditure, open to consideration on the part of the meeting. More important still is the census of membership read by the superintendent minister, and usually followed by an earnest conversation on the spiritual condition of the circuit.

All schemes for new chapels, schools, or houses must come before this meeting for sanction. Lay-agents employed in any society are under its oversight. The invitation of ministers, the reception of candidates for the ministry, the election of representatives to the Synod, proposals for the division of the circuit, education in day and Sunday schools, Temperance and Foreign Missions, the appointment of circuit officials, and, in brief, almost everything that concerns the well-being of the Church, must come before this united council for consideration.

And from first to last it is a gathering of those who are aiming at the advancement of the kingdom of Christ, and who are willing to give their personal service for that end.

Now, as we look again at the *personnel* of the meeting, it will be seen that it may be analysed into the following groups :—

1. The preachers, itinerant and lay ;

2. The stewards,—circuit, society, and poor stewards, responsible for the monies raised for the support of the ministry and for the care of the poor ;

3. The leaders or sub-pastors ;

4. The trustees, who have the care of the Church property ;

5. The Sunday - school representatives, who, with others present in virtue of various offices, are specially interested in the youth of the church.

In British Methodism, all these groups have also their separate councils, except the second and third groups, which are united in the Leaders' Meeting.

In the Methodist Episcopal Church of America the three classes of officers, leaders, stewards, and trustees, meet—(1) separately, under the chairmanship of the minister, for the transaction of business peculiarly their own ; (2) unitedly, as the *Official Board*, for mutual deliberation and administration ; and (3) once in three months, as a *Quarterly Conference*, under the chairmanship of the "presiding elder." This last-named gathering corresponds to the Quarterly Meeting in British Methodism.

But at every point, in the New World as in the Old, in the greater councils as in the less, you find *workers*. This basis of *work* is one of the great unconscious ideas that have shaped our organisation, and the clear recognition of it may help the development of the principle. That Church is the healthiest which finds most work for its members, and most frankly admits its workers into council.

It will be useful to note very briefly the character of the smaller circuit gatherings.

The *Local Preachers' Meeting* is also quarterly, and is a united gathering of the lay preachers of the circuit. Long before the "itinerant" became an "ordained" preacher, John Wesley's assistants had each his corps of "local" preachers, who followed their ordinary trades and pursuits, but gave what time they could spare to evangelistic service within the circuit. The earliest printed plan, containing the names of such volunteer helpers, goes back to 1777, and at the Conference of 1796 we first hear of the Local Preachers' Meeting. After the lapse of a whole century, at the Conference of 1896, legislation on the subject of lay preachers reached the high-water mark of completeness. The laws and usages of intervening years were gathered together, revised and codified, and with one or two more recent additions, constitute a code which is nearly ideal.

THE METHODIST PARISH

Probably few ever consider how large a proportion of the pulpits of Methodism are occupied week after week by laymen. Our indebtedness to these voluntary workers is powerfully illustrated by some interesting figures prepared in 1897 for the Local Preachers' Committee of the Bristol district. Three months were selected, and a careful calculation was made as to the number of services conducted by ministers and local preachers respectively. The following figures give the result :—

Number of chapels, 376.

Number of Sunday services for the three months, 8940.

Number of ministers, 101.

Number of local preachers, 852.

Number of services conducted by ministers, 1979.

Number conducted by local preachers, 6961.

No less than 77¾ per cent. of actual services during the three months were taken by laymen.

The proportion for the whole country would not be quite so high. According to a reliable estimate, five out of every seven sermons preached on a Sunday in Wesleyan churches in England and Wales are preached by local preachers. If on any given Sunday all local preachers *went out on strike*, the result would be disastrous. The big town churches would carry on their services as usual, but in country towns, agricultural villages, and mission-rooms, there would be, in most instances, no preacher. Without this vigorous lay army, we should be utterly unable to maintain the work of our Church in scores and hundreds of towns and villages.

The *Leaders' Meeting* is a gathering of *under-pastors.* In circuits where several churches are under the care of each minister, a sub-pastorate is absolutely necessary. The work done by curates in the Anglican Church, and by elders in the Presbyterian, is effected in Methodism by the grouping of members into classes, each of which is under the care of a leader. It is a method which has answered admirably in the past, and needs to-day not so much change as development.

The spiritual welfare of the Church, the contributions from the classes towards the support of the ministry, the administration of the Poor Fund, all come under review in the Leaders' Meeting. It is also a court of discipline to consider any charge that may be brought against a member of the Church.

The *Trustees' Meeting* is responsible for the property of the Church, for its care and maintenance, and for the carrying out of all schemes of extension sanctioned by the Quarterly Meeting. The duties of trustees, and the provisions of the Model Deed, are fully outlined in handbooks named in a later chapter.

The trustees do not own the property of which they have the care, but hold it in trust for the Wesleyan Methodist Church. It cannot be alienated, or handed over to another Church, and no preacher duly appointed can be excluded from its pulpits. At a meeting some years ago, with reference to Roman

Catholic property in Great Britain, the Methodist Model Deed was referred to by the late Cardinal Manning as the finest legal instrument he knew for the security of property for ecclesiastical purposes.

These four councils have constitutions definitely fixed and understood, and no deviation is permissible. In addition to these, the Sunday school has its Committee and Teachers' Meeting (though in these there is not uniformity), and the Wesley Guild has its executive, clearly defined by its constitution. These represent great interests which will more and more call for earnest and thoughtful attention.

The outline given in this chapter refers chiefly to the organisation of the Wesleyan Methodist Church. In the smaller Methodist Churches there are variations in detail, but most of the essential principles are the same. There is " variety of operation, but the same spirit."

XI.

THE CHURCH PRIN-CIPLES OF JOHN WESLEY

" A foolish consistency is the hob-goblin of little minds, adored by little statesmen and philosophers, and divines. With consistency a great soul has nothing to do. He may as well concern himself with his shadow on the wall."—EMERSON.

Was John Wesley a High Churchman? What he himself SAID —and DID.

THE CHURCH PRINCIPLES OF JOHN WESLEY

AGAIN and again ill-informed or disingenuous Anglicans have deliberately charged Methodists with unfaithfulness to their great leader. "John Wesley," they say, "was a Churchman, and a High Churchman, rigid in his adherence to the articles, the rubrics, the principles of Anglicanism. He would never have consented to the creation of a separate Church. Consequently all good Methodists who wish to be true to the spirit of Wesley himself, ought to return at once to the bosom of the mother Church."

Now the answer to the question, "Was John Wesley a High Churchman?" is (1) He was; and (2) He was not.

It is altogether a question of dates.

During his mission to Georgia, and previously, at Oxford, John Wesley was the highest of High Churchmen.

By a High Churchman I mean one who believes in apostolical succession, in the divine authority of Episcopacy, in the priestly idea of the Sacraments, and who attaches great importance to the details of ritual.

John Wesley was all that,—and more.

He read the prayers at five in the morning, and advocated fasting communion ; he enjoined fasting and confession ; he observed an old rubric requiring the baptism of children by immersion ; he rebaptized the children of Dissenters ; he refused to read the burial service over those who had not received Episcopalian baptism ; he repelled from the Lord's Table those who were not in communion with the Church of England. A Moravian, John Martin Boëlzius, a good man and devoted Christian, presented himself at the Sacrament of the Lord's Supper, and Wesley refused to administer the bread and wine to him, because he had not been baptized by a clergyman episcopally ordained. Referring to this incident in later years, Wesley said—

"Can anyone carry High Church zeal higher than this ! And how well have I since been beaten with my own staff !"

Up to the very moment of his leaving Georgia, John Wesley was unquestionably an extreme High Churchman.

But it is equally true that *from the day of the great spiritual change that took place in 1738, Wesley began, step by step, to unlearn and discard his High Churchism.*

The old superstitions fell away, one by one, like worn-out husks, pushed off by the new life within.

Seven years went by. They were, as we have seen, years of marvellous awakening. Wesley was carried along on the flood-tide of new spiritual life. He saw

156

the colliers of Kingswood, the smugglers of Cornwall, the roughs of Wednesbury, and the rabble of New-castle, changed, purified, transformed, not in churches, but in cottages and barns, in quarries and on open moors, not only through the instrumentality of his own preaching, but that of plain, unordained, unlettered men, whose only call was direct and divine. He learned that "God fulfils Himself in many ways." Throughout these strenuous years he was preaching, travelling, observing, reading, and thinking; and by the end of them, the divine right of bishops, apostolical succession, and the sacred obligation of rubrics, had all gone overboard.

To make the matter perfectly plain, it will be interesting to note first of all, *what John Wesley actually said* on these points, and, further, *what he did.*

And firstly, WHAT JOHN WESLEY SAID.

On *Episcopacy* this is his ripe and deliberate verdict.

"**As to my own judgment, I still believe 'the Episcopal form of Church government' to be scriptural and apostolical. I mean, well agreeing with the practice and writings of the apostles. But that it is prescribed in Scripture, I do not believe. This opinion, which I once zealously espoused, I have been heartily ashamed of ever since I read Bishop Stillingfleet's *Irenicon*. I think he has un=answerably proved that 'neither Christ nor His apostles prescribe any particular form of**

Church government; and that *the plea of Divine right for Diocesan Episcopacy was never heard of in the Primitive Church.*"

(*Works*, vol. xiii. p. 211.)

In a letter written in 1784, he still further says :

"Lord King's *Account of the Primitive Church* convinced me many years ago that *Bishops and Presbyters are the same order,* and consequently have the same right to ordain " (*Works*, vol. xiii. p. 251).

Apostolical Succession he describes in emphatic language as a broken chain.

"I deny that the Romish bishops came down by uninterrupted succession from the apostles. *I never could see it proved ; and, I am persuaded, I never shall.* . . . But, farther, it is a doctrine of your Church, that the intention of the administrator is essential to the validity of the sacraments which are administered by him. . . . If *you* pass for a priest, are you assured of the intention of the bishop that ordained you? If not, you may happen to be no priest, and so all your ministry is nothing worth ; nay, by the same rule, he may happen to be no bishop. And who can tell how often this has been the case? But if there has been only one such instance in a thousand years, what becomes of your *uninterrupted* succession ?"

(*Works*, vol. iii. pp. 44, 45.)

And in a letter written only a few years before his death, he reiterates this judgment in the plainest possible terms.

"I firmly believe I am a scriptural *episkopos* (or bishop) as much as any man in England or in Europe.   (*For the uninterrupted succession I know to be a fable, which no man ever did or can prove.*")

(Letter on the Church, dated August 19th, 1785. *Works*, vol. xiii. p. 253.)

As to *Rubric and Ritual*, he was led, step by step, and often against his will, to allow one innovation after another, until vast departures were made from the decorous traditions of the Anglican Church. Such practices as open-air preaching, and lay preaching especially, called forth the wrath of his contemporaries.   Secker, afterwards archbishop, bitterly attacked Wesley, and declared such practices to be—

"Oppositions to the most fundamental principles and essentially constituent parts of our Establishment."

In a letter dated April 10th, 1761, Wesley deals trenchantly with this statement, and his reply shows how far he had travelled since the days in Georgia.

"'The most fundamental principles!'   No more than the tiles are the most fundamental principles of a house.   Useful, doubtless, they are, yet you must take them off if you would repair the rotten timber beneath. 'Essentially constituent parts of our Estab=

lishment.' Well, we will not quarrel for a word. Perhaps the doors may be essentially constituent parts of the building we call a church. Yet if it were on fire we might innocently break them open, or even throw them for a time off the hinges. *Now this is really the case.* The timber is rotten, yea, the main beams of the house; and they want to place that firm beam, salvation by faith, in room of that rotten beam, salvation by works. A fire *is* kindled in the Church, the house of the living God; the fire of love of the world, ambition, covetousness, envy, anger, malice, bitter zeal, — in one word, of ungodliness and unrighteousness. Oh! who will come and help to quench it? Under dis= advantages and discouragements of every kind, a little handful of men have made a beginning, and I trust they will not leave off till the building is saved, or they sink in the ruins of it" (*Works*, vol. xiii. pp. 235–237).

On *Catholic Principles* Wesley became "exceeding broad."

"If by Catholic Principles, you mean any other than scriptural, they weigh nothing with me: I allow no other rule, whether of faith or practice, than the Holy Scriptures."

(*Works*, vol. i. p. 201.)

And he summed up the whole question in the words quoted by Richard Watson from a letter to Charles Wesley.

"**Church or no Church, we must attend to the work of saving souls.**"

(Letter to Charles Wesley, Watson's *Works*, vol. v. p. 199.)

But **WHAT JOHN WESLEY DID** was even more remarkable than what he said.

With a man of his character, to be convinced was to act.

He disregarded all parochial limitations.

He went straight to the people. They needed his message, and he laughed at all barriers. Methodism is sometimes described as a schism from the Anglican Church. Even so far as the leaders were concerned, it was not true, for they were practically forced out of it. But the vast majority of the early Methodists were never in the Church. The masses of the people were utterly neglected, and Wesley felt that their need was his opportunity. Within a little more than a year after the great spiritual crisis of his life, Wesley settled this point very definitely; and in a letter to a friend declared his intentions in a phrase which will never be forgotten.

"**Suffer me now to tell you my principles in this matter. I LOOK UPON ALL THE WORLD AS MY PARISH; thus far I mean, that, in whatever part of it I am, I judge it meet, right, and my bounden duty to declare, unto all that are willing to hear, the glad tidings of salvation**" (*Works*, vol. i. p. 201).

Wesley built chapels all over the land. Not one of them was consecrated. He never asked for consecration. And though at first they were intended to supplement, and not to supplant the services of the Church, yet their building was a daring transgression of parochial rights.

But even more significant than the absence of consecration, was the fact that some of Wesley's chapels were actually "licensed" as dissenting places of worship. The "New Room" at Bristol was licensed in 1748, and the Methodists were deliberately described in the document as "Protestant subjects *dissenting from the Church of England.*" That Wesley did this with his eyes open is evident from the vehement protest of Charles Wesley, with which the parchment is endorsed.

It is still more significant that *Wesley allowed unordained laymen to preach.* As we have seen, this step involved a great wrench on his part : "To touch this point," he says, "was to touch the apple of mine eye." But convinced that it was right and necessary, he never hesitated for a moment.

Another illustration of his detachment from his old ecclesiastical principles is the fact that he *revised the Thirty-Nine Articles.*

Yes, he deliberately shortened and modified them, and reduced them to twenty-five.

His omissions are suggestive, such as the following :—

    Article 8. The Three Creeds.

        ,,   17. Predestination and Election.

        ,,   20. The Authority of the Church.

        ,,   23. On Ministering to the Congregation.

Article 34. Altered as follows :—" Every particular Church may ordain changes, or abolish rites and ceremonies, so that all things be done to edification."

Article 36. Consecration of Bishops and Ministers.

But the climax was reached when *Wesley himself ordained men as bishops and presbyters.*

America was the first problem which led Wesley to take this step. The position was extraordinary. At the Revolution the Episcopalian establishment was abolished, and the religious institutions of the country were in chaos. Methodism had already taken root, but it needed care and development. There were fifteen thousand members, and eighty-three itinerant preachers, but as yet their forces were not organised. Twice Wesley tried to persuade Lowth, the Bishop of London, one of the most liberal men of the time, to ordain at least one of the preachers, so that the Sacraments might be administered to the people, but with no avail ; and, after long delay, Wesley determined to cut the knot in characteristic fashion.

In September, 1784, Wesley met Coke at Bristol, and ordained him as the *first bishop* of the Methodist Church in America ; and, at the same time, he ordained two other preachers as presbyters. On crossing the Atlantic, their first act was the ordination of Bishop Asbury, one of the heroes of the old American days.

It is interesting to remember that the Methodist bishops were the first Protestant bishops of the New World ; and the Methodist Episcopal Church, with a fair field and no favour, rapidly became the greatest Protestant community in the world.

But, the Rubicon once crossed, Wesley went even further.

At the Conference in London, in 1785, he ordained three preachers to administer the Sacraments in Scotland.

During the next year he extended the same privilege to Ireland and the West Indies.

In 1787, at the Manchester Conference, Mather, Rankin, and Moore were ordained, with authority to administer the Sacraments in any part of England. Mather received bishop's orders, though Wesley preferred to use the term "Superintendent." Every superintendent was a New Testament bishop in Wesley's eyes.

One step more was necessary, and it was taken when Wesley framed the *Deed of Declaration*, preparing the way for the existence of Methodism as a distinct Church. This was in 1784, prior to the above ordinations, but supreme in order of importance. Separation was contrary to his wish and early hope, but he saw that it must come. Only three years before his death he wrote—

"A kind of separation has already taken place, and will inevitably spread, though by slow degrees" (*Works*, vol. xiii. p. 264).

"Their enemies," he says again, "provoke them to it, the clergy in particular, most of whom, far from thanking them for continuing in the Church, use all the means in their power, fair and unfair, to drive them out of it " (*Works*, vol. xiii. p. 266).

Such were John Wesley's principles, acted upon with honesty and courage. It may safely be said that during his later years there is not a page, not a line, not a word, to show that he ever deviated from the convictions mainly arrived at in 1746. He was never bitter, always reasonable and conciliatory, unwilling to break away from old and venerable traditions, but when once a path opened out which he believed to be right, nothing could hold him back. And throughout, his attitude towards men who differed from him in opinion was always that expressed in his own fine words—

"**I desire to form a League, offensive and defensive, with every soldier of Jesus Christ.**"

XII.

THE FAITH OF A METHODIST

"Our wills are ours, we know not
    how;
Our wills are ours to make them
    thine."—In Memoriam.

"I am housed at Mr. Wildman's,
an old friend of mine in these parts;
he and his wife are two perfectly
honest Methodists.   When I came I
asked her after news, and she replied:
'Why, Mr. Tennyson, there's only one
piece of news that I know—that Christ
died for all men.'   And I said to her,
'That is old news, and good news,
and new news.'"
    Lord Tennyson in a letter to Miss
Sellwood, 1839.

> Methodism, with its
> message to ALL MEN,
> stands out against the
> background of Calvin-
> ism and Deism, — the
> one the prevailing theo-
> logical, as the other the
> philosophical creed of
> the eighteenth century.
> It is the religion of the
> **changed life,** based
> upon experience, and
> rooted in the Word of
> God.

THE FAITH OF A METHODIST

In Ian Maclaren's *Kate Carnegie and Those Ministers* there is a tremendous scene where Rabbi Saunderson, cut to the quick by the latitudinarian views of his young friend Carmichael, delivers his soul on the dread subject of the divine decrees. It had to be done. The inexorable logic of his creed drove him to do it, though the words had to be wrung out of his very heart's blood.

He took as his text "Vessels of wrath," and the congregation sat breathless with dread expectation, for the old man was loved and venerated, and his words went deep.

His divisions, announced after a grave introduction on the Divine Sovereignty, were—"'First,'—and between the heads the Rabbi paused, as one whose breath failed him—'every man belongs absolutely to God by his creation.' 'Second. The purpose of God about each man precedes his creation.' 'Third. Some are destined to Salvation, and some to Damnation.' 'Fourth,'—here the hard breathing became a sob—'each man's lot is unto the glory of God.'"

Men went white and women trembled as he developed his theme, and they gazed fascinated at the preacher as, with painful determination, he enforced the idea of absolute divine supremacy.

"It is as a sword piercing the heart to receive this truth, but it is a truth and must be believed. There are hundreds of thousands in the past who were born and lived and died, and were damned, for the glory of God. There are hundreds of thousands in this day who have been born and are living and shall die, and be damned, for the glory of God. There are hundreds of thousands in the future who shall be born and shall live and shall die, and shall be damned, for the glory of God. All according to the will of God, and none shall dare say nay nor change the purpose of the Eternal."

Then the flickering lamps go out. Only two are left, and they smoulder down into darkness as the Rabbi slowly forces out his last words.

"Shall . . . not . . . the Judge of all the earth . . . do . . . right?"

He finishes, and a great sigh echoes through the church; and out of the silence a woman's voice ejaculates, "God have mercy upon us."

Round the old Rabbi is thrown all the glamour of Ian Maclaren's wonderful pathos; we love him in spite of his rigid views, as John Carmichael did, and it is well, perhaps, that we should be made to feel how true men *could* so believe and still hold fast to God. But it is undeniable that "the robust Calvinism with which every Scot is saturated," found, in days gone by, expression just as uncompromising as in the Rabbi's sermon.

But it is even more important for us to remember that **Calvinism,** more or less modified, was, speaking generally, the working creed of orthodox Christianity in the eighteenth century, and, when Wesley began his work, Calvinism practically meant predestination, election, and reprobation.

Calvinism is, of course, not to be dismissed with a scoff at the extreme views so terribly expressed in the Scotch sermon. As a philosophic system of theology, it has both dignity and grandeur. In breadth of conception, strength, and consistency it stands unrivalled. God is supreme. The divine will is everything. The divine nature is the focus around which all other thoughts of man and the universe crystallise. It produced great men and powerful preachers. Whitefield himself was a Calvinist; Berridge, Toplady, and Rowland Hill were all men of power; while Robert Hall and Spurgeon, in later times, are evidence of a strength in the creed which no elements of error can belittle. It was, indeed, utterly removed from some flabby and sentimental theories of modern times, in which God's will counts for little, and adoration and reverence are scarcely recognised at all. What we urgently need in the reshaping of theology to-day is a philosophy of religion just as vigorous and logical as Calvinism, but more generous in its conception of the divine nature. With the doctrine of the divine sovereignty we have no quarrel, and from larger views of God will issue nobler views of human life.

But when Wesley began his work, the *accidents* of Calvinism had become the *essentials*. Predestinarianism was relentlessly taught, both from Anglican and Nonconformist pulpits, and the hard repulsive theory of the divine decrees, finally and inexorably determining man's destiny, paralysed evangelism and deadened the spiritual life of the Church.

But the widespread apathy of Wesley's time had another and deeper cause. If Calvinism was the popular theology, **Deism** was the philosophic creed of the time. No doubt it was to some extent a reaction against the severer forms of Calvinism as taught in the seventeenth century, but in Wesley's day it was a distinct force to be reckoned with, and one of the most deadly character. Bishop Butler, its most powerful opponent, in a charge to his Durham clergy, boldly declared that "as different ages have been distinguished by different sorts of particular errors and vices, the deplorable distinction of ours is an avowed scorn of religion in some, and a growing disregard to it in the generality." Bishop Warburton, a man of altogether different character, said, with equal emphasis, "I have lived to see what law-givers have always seemed to dread, as the certain prognostic of public ruin, that fatal crisis when religion hath lost its hold on the minds of a people." This "great growth of atheism and infidelity," as Hartley, the physician, described it, was undoubtedly due to the subtle ridicule poured upon religion by the Deists, whose baleful influence was exerted, not so much in open warfare, as in scoffing irony and contempt. Freethinking became popular, and the most sacred beliefs were discussed with no little sceptical bias in drawing-rooms, coffee-houses, taverns, and all places of public resort. It is no wonder, then, that in the absence of any inspiring view of religion, and stifled by this atmosphere of unbelief, the pulpit almost ceased to be a power. There was no vigorous conviction behind its teachings. There were good and scholarly men in the Church of England, but their sermons had " no teeth." The fashionable exquisites and well-dressed sensualists of the day could attend church without the least fear of discomfort. The one great dread of the average preacher was lest he should be accused of zeal. Polite, agreeable discourses that disturbed nobody, were the order of the day, and though Hogarth's *Sleeping Congregation* may be a caricature, we may be sure that in some cases it was not far from the truth.

Against the background of a perverted Calvinism, then, and even more clearly against the apathy and irreligion due to the Deistical philosophy of the period, the faith of the early Methodists stands out in bold relief. They boldly and definitely taught that—

All men **need** to be saved ; that

All men **may** be saved ; that

All men may **know** themselves saved ; and that

All men may be saved to the **uttermost.**

To us these propositions are truisms ; but if we would understand Methodism, we must remember that they were all either doubted or denied. The first was controverted by the shallow philosophy of the time, with its easy-going views of human nature ; the second was in direct opposition of the commonly accepted creed of a limited salvation; while even the worthiest theologians and preachers of the time held it doubtful whether any can know themselves saved, and highly improbable that men can be saved to the uttermost save in the very hour and article of death.

Now these four principles stated above stand for the four cardinal doctrines accentuated by Methodism—

> **Original sin,**
> **Universal redemption,**
> **The witness of the Spirit,** and
> **Scriptural holiness.**

But though distinctive enough in the eighteenth century, they are by no means distinctive to-day. I have painted in the lurid background of error and unbelief, and have emphasised the predestinarianism of the time, to show how much they were needed then, but the evangelical revival has so leavened all Churches, that it is difficult to find a man who still holds the old theory of election and reprobation. Religion to-day, if it be real, is invariably respected. The Calvinism of our time has nobler views of God, and its teaching has mellowed and deepened. It is not dead, but has cast off excrescences which two hundred years ago were so prominent that they were mistaken for the creed itself.

But there is none the less need for the Methodist witness. Other Churches may be needed to emphasise their own special vision of truth, but it is our chief mission to preach deliverance, pardon, and holiness for every soul of man.

The central thought of Methodism, therefore, is the

changed life. It is the religion of the **healthy soul.** It holds that it is not necessary for a man to go limping all his days, or be hampered by taints of spiritual disease, which lower the moral tone and destroy the joy of life. He may be strong, vigorous, and free. Sin to the early Methodists was a terrible reality. The Deism of the day ignored sin, and ridiculed the idea of a man whimpering and groaning about the state of his soul. But to the preachers of the Great Revival, who knew men's hearts as few ever have done, sin was a disease, and a disease to be extirpated. It was not merely to be alleviated and kept under. It was to be conquered and cast out.

And in harmony with this strong conception of sin, holiness with Wesley was simply healthiness, a sane and natural meaning of the word. He taught his followers to sing—

> " The seed of sin's disease,
>   Spirit of **health** remove—
>   Spirit of finished holiness,
>   Spirit of perfect love."

His declared aim was to " spread scriptural holiness "— scriptural healthiness—" throughout the land." Nor was there anything earthy, narrow, or accommodating about this conception of the ideal life. Holiness meant nothing less than a soul flooded, drenched, penetrated by a divine life that would cast out everything lower than itself.

> " Send us the Spirit of Thy Son,
>   To make the depths of Godhead known,
>   To make us share the *life divine*."

The last line of the verse quoted above suggests the characteristic idea under which holiness was conceived. It was **perfect love.** " Pure love reigning alone in the heart and life; this," said Wesley, "is the whole of Christian perfection." And it was, first and foremost, a consuming love for God. The Christian is a God-possessed man; and if we would know what such a mighty love can do for a man, and how it issues, not in dreamy mysticism or narrow pietism, but in the raising to its highest power every noble human faculty, in the opening out of a life of infinite progress and ever more glorious possibilities, we must read the inspiring series of hymns, " On Seeking for Full Redemption," and then study the lives of the brave and saintly men to whom such hymns came with the force and freshness of a new revelation.

It is necessary now to see how the faith of the Methodist is related to **Catholic truth** in general, and to **the principles of Protestantism** in particular.

Our doctrine of God is that of the great Creeds—
" God, in Three Persons, blessed Trinity."
Indeed, in so brief a summary as the present, it is almost sufficient to say, so far as this aspect of our subject is concerned, that every Methodist accepts the Apostle's Creed as an evidence that he is "one in faith and doctrine" with "Christians of every land and age."

But the doctrine of the Trinity in a very special

manner was the very root and inspiration of all Methodist teaching, and, since the days of the early Christian martyrs, it has perhaps never received such striking expression as in the life and thought and song of the early Methodists. In the very beautiful group of hymns in the old hymn-book headed "Believer's Rejoicing," no less than eighteen are ascriptions of praise to Father, Son, and Spirit; and some were among the most joyous hymns of gladness inspired by the Great Revival.

In the four characteristic truths of the Methodist faith already named, while the first emphasises the fact of sin, the other three powerfully illustrate the idea of the Trinity as involved in the work of salvation—redemption through the Son; assurance through the Holy Spirit; and holiness, "perfect love," which is also perfect childhood, through faith in the living Father. And so **GOD** in all His perfection becomes ours, a thought beautifully expressed in one of the hymns just referred to—

> "A thousand oracles divine
>   Their common beams unite,
> That sinners may with angels join
>   To worship God aright;
> To praise a Trinity adored
>   By all the hosts above,
> And one thrice-holy God and Lord
>   Through endless ages love.
>
> Triumphant host! they never cease
>   To laud and magnify
> The Triune God of holiness,
>   Whose glory fills the sky;

Whose glory to this earth extends,
    When God Himself imparts,
**And the whole Trinity descends
Into our faithful hearts."**

If, further, we are asked **where we get our authority** for the truths we teach, we are at one with Protestantism in making our appeal to Scripture and experience.

The Bible is our Rule of Faith. The faith of the Methodist rests upon **the solid rock of Scripture.** It is built upon the foundation of the apostles and prophets. As life passed, Wesley's keen intellect cut deep down through all human creeds, forms, and confessions, to the very heart of the Word itself. There, and there only, he found a complete answer to the mysterious problem of life.

One of the most striking passages in Wesley's writings is the one in which he declares himself to be a "man of one book"; and which, for intensity of feeling and noble expression, and for reverent sense of the mystery of human life, might stand beside some of the greatest words ever spoken.

" To candid, reasonable men I am not afraid to lay open what have been the inmost thoughts of my heart. I have thought, I am a creature of a day, passing through life as an arrow through the air. I am a spirit come from God, and returning to God; just hovering over the great gulf, till, a few moments hence, I am no more seen; I drop into an unchangeable eternity! I want to know one thing, the way to heaven; how to land safe on that happy shore. God Himself has condescended to teach the way; for this very end He came down from heaven. He hath written it down in a book. Oh, give me that book! at any price, give me the Book of God! I have it; here is knowledge enough for me. Let me be *homo unius libri*. Here, then, I am far from the busy ways of men. I sit down alone; only God is here. In His presence I open, I read His Book, for this end—to find the way to heaven. Is there a doubt concerning the meaning of what I read? Does anything appear dark or intricate? I lift my heart to the Father of lights. 'Lord, is it not Thy Word?' If any man lack wisdom, let him ask it of God. Thou givest liberally and upbraidest not. Thou hast said, if any man be willing to do Thy will, he shall know. I am willing to do; let me know Thy will."

Side by side with the Bible we place **Experience**. The Holy Spirit's inward witness to the truth is the supreme positive authority of Protestantism.

It is curious that Luther's writings had so much to do with the enlightenment of both Charles and John Wesley. The passage from Luther's *Commentary on the Galatians*, which so greatly helped the younger brother, is full of the spirit of assurance which sounded so clearly in the early days of Methodism. "Read these most sweet and comfortable words," he says, " 'Who loved *me*, and gave Himself for *me*,' and so inwardly practice with thyself that thou with a sure faith mayest conceive and print this *me* upon thy heart and apply it to thyself, not doubting that thou art of the number to whom this *me* belongeth; also, that Christ hath not only loved Peter and Paul, and given Himself for them, but that the same grace also which is comprehended in this *me* cometh unto us as unto them."

And John Wesley's own power began on that fateful day when he too grasped this powerful truth, when religion became for him a matter of experience, and he was able for the first time to say, " I felt that I did trust in Christ, in Christ alone for salvation." From that time forward he boldly preached, to cultured and ignorant alike, a full, free, immediate, instantaneous deliverance, — a deliverance which meant new power of life in the soul, upward in its tendency, touching the whole man, issuing in a consecration of every power of body, soul, and spirit unto God. Every true Methodist could say with St. John, " That which we have seen and heard declare we unto you also, that ye also may have fellowship with us."

The hymns of early Methodism ring again with this personal note. Dr. William Taylor, of America, tells how, when he was a boy, he once heard a sermon on "appropriating faith." His first question on getting home was, "Father, what *is* appropriating faith?"—a circumstance not very complimentary to the preacher. His father replied, " My boy, take your Bible and underline all the *me's* and *my's* and the *mine's*, and you will soon find out what 'appropriating faith' is."

If the *me's*, *my's*, and *mine's* were underscored in Charles and John Wesley's hymns, it would show better than anything else the intense personal force behind the Great Revival.

And out of the glow of Experience,—**Evangelism.** With the early Methodists it was only one step from "*me*" to the "*world*." With deep and reverent faith he would sing—

> "Lord, I believe Thy precious blood,
>   Which at the mercy seat of God,
> For ever doth for sinners plead,
>   For **me**, even for **my soul** was shed."

But instantly the mind flings itself out to the uttermost limits of the human race. The gift received is a gift for all, and the missionary spirit of Methodism finds glorious expression in the very next stanza—

> "Lord, I believe were sinners more
>   Than sands upon the ocean shore,
> Thou hast for **all** a ransom paid,
>   For **all** a full atonement made."

It is not a little remarkable that these two verses, which I have instinctively quoted, are from a Moravian hymn translated by John Wesley, a hymn which adds another link to the spiritual genealogy traced in an earlier chapter. The Moravian Church is the mother of modern Protestant Foreign Missions, and the debt ought to be fully and gratefully acknowledged. The hymn is Count von Zinzendorf's "Christi Blut und Gerechtigheit," composed in 1739, the supreme year of the Methodist movement, during his journey home from the West Indies. Wesley published his translation in "Hymns and Sacred Poems" the following year. It was, therefore, one of the earliest hymns to sound the great evangelistic and missionary note from end to end of the land.

And now, gathering together these thoughts into one focus, we shall see that the faith of the Methodist finds its natural expression in **Fellowship.**

In a creed which finds in Perfect Love its ideal of the Holy Life there is no room for selfishness. For those who heartily believe the whole law to be summed up in the commandment, "Thou shalt love,"—first "the Lord thy God," and then "thy neighbour as thyself,"—there is a magnetism which, as has been shown in an earlier chapter, draws men together, and creates for itself new modes of communion. Fellowship is of the very essence of Methodism, the fibre of its organisation, the resultant of the truths most emphasised in its teaching.

And in fellowship we find the basis of the Methodist conception of the **Church.** In the last chapter we saw how Wesley, step by step, was led to abandon his early High Church theories, and to seek more scriptural forms of Church organisation. But the positive theory which supplanted the discarded ideas was never definitely formulated. The new conception was a growth. Methodism was unconsciously a Church long before it assumed the name. But to-day it is possible to define our position, and it cannot

be done more simply or clearly than in the words of
Dr. Findlay, "To us the Church is not the priesthood,
the ritual, the form of Sacrament or government : it is
the *Society of Jesus*. We find its germ-cell in the little
company of brother disciples gathered round the
Master in common talk and at a common table.
The entire aggregate of the Christian Church throughout the world is formed by the repetition, multiplica-
tion, and reproduction in ten thousand varied forms
of that germ-cell : it is the development of the
original communion of Christ and His spiritual
brethren . . . The Church is the body of the
recognised citizens of the Divine Kingdom."

The conception embodied in these two sentences,
of the Church as **" a society "—" of citizens,"**
perfectly harmonises with the idea suggested in the
word **" ecclesia "** so frequently used in the New
Testament.

It is a Greek word with an interesting history.
Literally it means the " called out," and it was the
name given to the great council, open to all free
citizens, and in which they discussed and managed
their own affairs. The Greek, always proud of his
citizenship, never more fully realised its meaning than
when he met his fellow-citizens in the " ecclesia."
And in that powerful assembly three ideas were ever
recognised. As citizens they felt the bond of a
common life, they shared *common ideals*, and they
joined in *common worship*, for special religious rites
were always associated with the *ecclesia*.

These three ideas are equally characteristic of the

fellowship of the Christian Church. It is a community of people who have found a common life in Christ, who bear witness to common ideals of faith and holiness, and who find common ground in worship.

But in the Christian " ecclesia " the order is completely reversed. Worship takes the first place. We meet in the ever-hallowed name of the Father, and our recognition of our common life and common testimony springs naturally from that relationship. The early Christians " were accustomed to meet on a stated day," said Pliny in his letter to Trajan, "and sing a hymn to Christ as God," and in such simple worship they realised that they were a " kingdom of priests," united by the holiest of ties. What was a mere formality in other assemblies was an intense reality to them. The divine presence and love overpowered and governed all other ideas. And, from the very beginning, the sacred rites in which Christian men and women most deeply recognise their common citizenship were *the two Sacraments*, Baptism and the Lord's Supper : the one witnessing to the life to which in Christ all men are called, and the other to the truths of salvation through faith in which we possess that life, and of which we are living witnesses.

Both are essential to a complete Christian fellowship, for in the one rite we claim the unconscious little ones for the Kingdom, and in the other, as intelligent believers in Christ, we recognise in the most sacred manner possible our oneness with Him. It is an interesting fact that in the early days of Methodism the Sacraments were greatly prized by the people, and one of the strongest demands, which Wesley found it very difficult to resist, and which at length he partially gratified, was that they should receive the Sacraments in their own houses of worship, and from the hands of their own ministers. The fellowship, which is of the essence of the Church, demanded it.

Such then, in brief and imperfect outline, is the faith of a Methodist, but this living, experimental, scriptural creed by no means exhausts the contents of Methodist teaching. There is a catholicity about Methodism which claims the whole Empire of Truth. Every great word that may stir the soul and uplift the life may be spoken from its pulpits. It welcomes light from every quarter, and in each successive age it is the work of its preachers to find new and vivid expression in the living language of the people of the deep things of God. But the truths emphasised in this chapter are fundamental, and can only be laid by as useless when sin has ceased to exist.

Yet there is need for largeness of view and intensity of purpose. The lives of men are wider and more complicated, their interests innumerable, and there is need that the old faith should take possession of the new fields.

There is nobility in the devotion of the olden days, even if the life of the eighteenth century was narrower than our own. As Miss Fowler has finely expressed it in *Isabel Carnaby* :—

" The Methodists of the past generation lived always with their lamps lit and their loins girded, as those that wait for their Lord; and they sought so diligently for the True that they had no leisure to look for the Beautiful, for it had not yet been revealed to them that the True and the Beautiful are one. They were so fearful of confounding the substance with the shadow, that they did not altogether realise that the shadow is, after all, but the reflection of the substance, and therefore a revelation of the same; and they gazed so steadfastly into heaven that they were in danger of forgetting how God made the earth as well as the heavens, and saw that it was good. To their ears there was no message in the wind, or the earthquake, or the fire; but they heard clearly the still small Voice, and they did whatsoever it commanded them."

For us new worlds have dawned. Art, science, and literature have opened to men fields of thought unknown to the wisest of our forefathers. We live at the end of the telephone, and can feel the throb of the big world as readily as a Methodist of the old time could know the doings of his quiet village. It is no use trying to narrow our lives so as to make religion easier. It cannot be done. If we even attempt to do it, we drop out of the march of humanity. What we need is not a smaller life, but a bigger religion, faith raised to a higher power, consecration more intelligent and larger in comprehension. "Christians of old," it has been said by a present-day writer, "lived in a bare and narrow room, but the fire of faith was sufficient to warm it. If you enlarge the room as you are doing, if you throw into it one space after another till it is a great hall, it follows that the fire must be increased. And it must be the true fire that is used to warm it, not a fire kindled of the world."

There is not only still need for the old Methodist fire: what we really need is *more* of it, to send a bright glow through the whole atmosphere of the modern world. " Religion, not a corner of life ; not life narrowed down ; but life more abundant, filling and illuminating *every interest* of body, soul, and spirit." That, and nothing less, is the ideal of faith for the twentieth century.

XIII.

ITINERARIES OF THOUGHT

*" A well-judging man will open his
trunk-line of study in such a direction
that, while habitually adhering to it,
he may enjoy a ready access to such
other fields of knowledge as are most
nearly related to it."*

SIR JAMES STEPHEN.

*Lines of study to be
followed by those who
wish to extend their
knowledge of Method-
ism, with notes on the
books to be read.*

ITINERARIES OF THOUGHT

IN making a real study of a special subject, the first question that arises is, from what point to set out, and the second, along what lines to travel. This little volume is intended simply as a point of departure, and it will be well perhaps to indicate in a closing chapter some of the routes that may be followed in further exploration. A great purpose will be served if others are stirred to thorough and extensive reading on some of the topics suggested. We have among us a number of Wesley experts, and their ranks might usefully be increased ; but it is desirable that among such experts, in addition to men of patient antiquarian research, we should have students of historical and philosophical bent, who will follow up some of the threads that the foregoing chapters only indicate.

Some, no doubt, will not have the time to follow any of the extended courses outlined below. For them I would suggest simply—

Lelièvre's "Life of Wesley" (New Edition. 7s. 6d.).

Findlay's "Church of Christ as set forth in the New Testament" (1s.). A small book, but invaluable as defining the Methodist position.

ITINERARIES

Overton's " **Evangelical Revival in the Eigh-teenth Century** " (2s. 6d.). An admirable and fair-minded survey of the whole Movement.

The groups of books that follow are not intended to be exhaustive, but rather suggestive, contributions to a larger Bibliography of the subject than has yet been attempted. The arrangement of topics proceeds from broader to more specialised reading : first the history of the century in which Wesley lived, then his Life, and, following it in natural order, the History of the Methodist Church. These are preliminary to such byways of study as the history of the Moravian Church, and to topics of such great importance as the Methodist conception of the Church, and the machinery of Methodism.

I. WESLEY'S ENVIRONMENT

" **Outlines of the World's History.** " By San-derson. Part IV. Modern History. (Blackie ; 2s. 6d.). Chapter IV., on the eighteenth century, is an admirable sketch of the world-events of Wesley's time. It is interesting to know that during Wesley's early years, Peter the Great was raising Russia to a formidable position among the nations ; Frederick of Prussia, "the greatest sovereign of the eighteenth century," was practically Wesley's contemporary, being born only ten years later ; George Washington, during the same period, was raised up to steer the American colonies through the dangerous years of their early independence. The same century witnessed the decline of the Turkish Empire, and the terrors of the French Revolution, a political earthquake which shook the whole of Europe.

Among famous men of the period are Benjamin Franklin, Emanuel Swedenborg, Laplace the astronomer, and Immanuel Kant the great metaphysician. The names of Galvani, Volta, Lavoisier, and Fahrenheit are all suggestive of discoveries of immense value to the race. Goethe and Schiller, Rousseau and Voltaire, were foremost in the world of European literature. Bach, Handel, Hadyn, and Mozart, all did their best work during Wesley's life. It was an age of movement preparatory to the great expansion of the nineteenth century.

"A Short History of the English People." By John Richard Green (Macmillan & Co.; 8s. 6d.). The appearance of this work marked a new departure in historical method. History in Green's hands, instead of being little more than a record of battle and conquest, became a mirror to the life of the people. One of the most notable features of the volume when first published was the space devoted to the study of Wesley and the Methodist Revival. Green's estimate ought not to be overlooked by any earnest student of Methodism.

Lecky's "History of the Eighteenth Century."—Vols. III. and IV. (Longmans, Green, & Co.; 36s. the 2 vols.). It is not a little remarkable that Mr. Lecky, one of the most thoughtful and impartial historians of the century, should devote one hundred and fifty pages to the rise of Methodism. Mr. Lecky in some respects grasps the philosophy of Methodism as scarcely any other writer does. Naturally, by a historian of rationalistic tendency, the extraordinary physical manifestations and the supposed credulity of Wesley are unduly emphasised. Yet Mr. Lecky speaks of Wesley as "one of the most powerful and most active intellects in England." And giving full value to "the career of the elder Pitt, and the splendid victories by sea and land that were won under his ministry," he declares that "they must yield in real importance to that religious revolution which shortly before had been begun in England by the preaching of the Wesleys and of Whitefield." An independent testimony such as this is of great value.

"**The Evangelical Revival in the Eighteenth Century.**"—Epochs of Church History. By Canon Overton (Longmans, Green, & Co., 1886 ; 2s. 6d.). Canon Overton has studied Wesley and his times very sympathetically, and, though writing from the Anglican standpoint, he is always conspicuously fair in spirit. This little volume treats of the Methodist Revival as part of a larger evangelical movement. The chapter on "The Doctrines of the Revival" is particularly useful.

"**The English Church in the Eighteenth Century.**" By Abbey and Overton (Longmans, 1887 ; 7s. 6d.). A study of life and thought in the Church of England from the Anglican point of view.

"**Religion in England under Queen Anne and the Georges.**"—Ecclesiastical History, vols. V., VI., and VII. By Dr. Stoughton (Hodder & Stoughton ;

8 vols., £3). Full of uncommon information and enriched by many wise and judicious estimates of men
and events. Dr. Stoughton is particularly helpful in his
portraiture of Nonconformists and Nonconformity.

"**History of English Thought in the Eighteenth Century.**" By Leslie Stephen. (2 vols., 28s.)
A book in which the movement is surveyed from the
standpoint of thought and literature. Considerable
attention is given to Methodism.

In addition to these, a study may be made of contemporary literature. It is too large a subject to be
even outlined here, but those who wish to understand
the life of the time should be familiar with such
works as "**The Spectator**" (2s.), *Boswell's* "**Life
of Johnson**" (2s. 6d.), *Hannah More's* "**Life
and Letters,**" the "**Letters of Mrs. Delany**"
(7s. 6d.), formerly Mary Granville, with whom Wesley
corresponded while at Oxford, and similar works.
Hogarth's Engravings, and, for those to whom
they are accessible, the original paintings in the
National Gallery, are deeply interesting as illustrating
the life of the period. **George Morland's** paintings
may be studied with the same intent ; idylls of home
and country life in the same century.

2. THE LIFE OF WESLEY

"**Wesley's Journal.**"—(Charles H. Kelly.) Of
this there are several editions, and others in preparation.

1. "***The One Volume Journal,***" uniform with

this volume, omitting only the long disquisitions, and such portions of the story as are of lesser interest.

2. *"The Two Volume Journal,"* with introduction by the Rev. W. L. Watkinson (2 vols., 7s.).

3. *"The Four Volume Journal"* (Students' Edition, 10s.).

4. *"The Library Edition of the Journal,"* with valuable annotations. This is now being prepared by the Rev. W. L. Watkinson, and, when complete, will be a work of national interest.

Lives of Wesley. A full list of Biographies and Biographical Notices has been published by the Wesley Historical Society. Here it is only necessary to mention a few of varying character. They are placed under the name of the author.

Lelièvre.—(Charles H. Kelly; 7s. 6d.) One of the best all-round lives. The new edition translated by a brother of the author, is admirably done.

Tyerman.—(Hodder & Stoughton, 1870. Out of print.) The most elaborate attempt at a complete biography yet made, but it falls far short of what is needed. There are the *materials* for a biography, but many of the estimates founded upon them will have to be modified by more recent studies and further discoveries.

Southey.—(Warne & Co.; 2s.) The first great Life of Wesley from an independent standpoint. It was published in 1820, and in some points gave rise to great controversy. Southey regarded *ambition* to be one of the leading motives of Wesley's character, a judgment he afterwards entirely reversed in a letter reproduced in facsimile in Dr. Smith's "History of Methodism."

Overton.—(Methuen & Co., 1891; 3s. 6d.) Canon Overton was for many years rector of Epworth, and devoted immense time and labour to the study of the Movement and the century. It is one of the most sympathetic pictures from the pen of an outsider yet printed.

Snell.—World's Epoch-Makers (T. & T. Clark, 1900; 3s.). There are many curious byways of thought and information in Mr. Snell's volume, but the "Epoch-making" character of John Wesley's work is just what he seems to miss. It adds little of value to the study of the Movement from a national stand-point.

Telford.—(Charles H. Kelly, 1886; 5s.) One of the best shorter lives, careful and accurate. Mr. Telford has also published a Penny Life and a Penny History, which have had a large circulation.

Wedgwood.—(Macmillan & Co., 1850. Out of print.) Miss Wedgwood's "John Wesley and the Evangelical Reaction of the Eighteenth Century," deserves to be read by every student of the Movement. For breadth of conception, and grasp of the significance of events, it ranks highly. It is not a systematic biography, but a series of philosophical studies. It merits far greater attention than it has yet received.

There are other interesting studies by Dr. Rigg, the Rev. Richard Green, and others.

3. THE HISTORY OF METHODISM

Histories, again, are so numerous that only a few of the more important can be named.

Smith, "History of Wesleyan Methodism." —George Smith, LL.D., F.A.S. (15s.) In three volumes, dealing respectively with "Wesley and his Times," "The Middle Age," and "Modern Methodism." It was first published in 1857, but there have been more recent editions. It is our standard history down to the year 1849.

Stevens, "The History of the Religious Movement of the Eighteenth Century, called Methodism."—Abel Stevens, LL.D. (3 vols., 10s. 6d.) A valuable survey, strong in biographical sketches of the men of Methodism, and in summaries of its progress decade by decade.

Hurst, "The History of Methodism." — John Fletcher Hurst, D.D., LL.D. (Charles H. Kelly, 1901 ; 3 vols., 25s.). This is a work on ambitious lines, originally intended to cover—(1) British Methodism, (2) American Methodism, and (3) World-wide Methodism. The three volumes on British Methodism are published at the Wesleyan Methodist Book-Room. They are profusely and beautifully illustrated. Some of the reproductions of famous paintings, and photogravures of drawings done specially for the work, are of great merit. The three volumes are crowded with interesting information. The facts are well grouped, and there is a great amount of new material. It is a work which ought to find a place in every library, public and private. The style is attractive, and for a history of British Methodism at once thoroughly popular and accurate, scarcely anything better can be desired.

"American Methodism." By Abel Stevens, LL.D. (Wesleyan Methodist Book-Room, 1885 : 3s. 6d.). A shorter history compiled from the author's "History of the Methodist Episcopal Church."

"Wesley and his Preachers, Their Con= quest of Britain." By G. Holden Pike. (Fisher Unwin ; 7s. 6d.) A recent work, brightly and effectively written, and showing careful study of an extensive field of Wesley literature.

"A Short History of the People called Methodists." By W. H. Daniels. (Hodder & Stoughton.) Especially good on the work in America.

"A History of Methodism in Ireland." By C. H. Crookshank, M.A. (Wesleyan Methodist Book-Room, 1888 ; 3 vols.)

4. MORAVIANS AND METHODISTS

"A Short History of the Moravian Church." By J. E. Hutton, M.A. (Moravian Publication Office). This little handbook is everything that could be desired : scholarly, accurate, and interesting from cover to cover. It is divided into two parts—(1) The Ancient Church, and (2) The Renewed Church. The two chapters on "The Beginning of Missions," and "The Brethren in England," are especially valuable.

"**The Beginnings of the Brethren's Church in England.**" By Gerard A. Wauer (translated by John Elliott). Published at the Moravian House, Baildon, Shipley; and at Fetter Lane. 1s.

"**The Dawn of the Reformation.**"—Vols. I. and II. "The Age of Wicliff," and "The Age of Hus," by Herbert B. Workman, M.A. (Charles H. Kelly. Vol. i. 2s. 9d.; vol. ii. 3s. 6d.). These two volumes ought to be read by any who want thoroughly to understand the origin of the Moravian Church and its true place in history. They are not only clear and attractive in style, but models of what Church History ought to be. Mr. Workman has a fine faculty for seeing to the heart of events.

5. THE METHODIST IDEA OF THE CHURCH

On this subject the literature is not great in quantity, but excellent in quality.

"**The Church of Christ as set forth in the New Testament.**" By G. G. Findlay, B.A., D.D. (Charles H. Kelly, 1893; 1s.). This little volume should be the text-book of any who wish to make a special study of this topic. It consists of two lectures delivered a few years ago to the young Methodists of Leeds at the request of the Leeds Methodist Council. Every thoughtful young Methodist ought to possess the book, which only costs one shilling. The lectures are clear as crystal, rich in New Testament thought and feeling, and deeply convincing. A more beautiful ideal of the Church we need not seek, for it is the ideal of Christ and His apostles. This invaluable little work ought to be read by tens of thousands in Great Britain, America, and in all parts of our Empire.

"**John Wesley and Modern 'Church Teaching.'**" By G. R. Osborn. A small 2d. booklet gathering together into one focus Wesley's own words on Church principles. The reading of this pamphlet would open the eyes of some of those who talk great nonsense about John Wesley's High Churchmanship. In every case the compiler quotes chapter and verse, so that no possible doubt can be felt as to the accuracy of the quotation.

"**Was John Wesley a High Churchman?**" A Dialogue. By Dr. Rigg. Published at 1d.

In several villages I have known where high Anglican rectors were trying to persuade their parishioners that John Wesley was a sympathiser with their own extreme views, the fallacy has been effectively exploded by the circulation of this little booklet. The arguments are plain and irrefutable.

"**Handbook of Scriptural Church Principles.**" By Dr. Gregory. (Wesleyan Methodist Book-Room; 1s.) A helpful Manual crowded with New Testament teaching. Some chapters, such as the one on "The Power of the Keys," are highly instructive.

"**Methodism in the Light of the Early Church.**" By W. F. Slater, M.A. 2s. 6d.

6. THE MACHINERY OF METHODISM

The subject of Methodist polity is a very wide one, and one where it is easy to go astray. Happily we have specialists who have made the subject their own, and I am able to add to the list of books suggested some deeply interesting notes from the pen of the Rev. John S. Simon. Some of the rarer books are also included in the list at his suggestion. With Mr. Simon's help I have endeavoured to make the outline valuable to young ministers who wish to master the polity of their own Church.

It is scarcely necessary to say that this special study must follow and be accompanied by a study of Methodist History. Our institutions can only be truly interpreted in the light of the events which led to their adoption. Such, indeed, is the principle which underlies the whole of the present volume.

1. *Text Books*—

"**Handbook of Wesleyan Methodist Polity and History.**" By the Rev. Benjamin Gregory, D.D. (Wesleyan Methodist Book-Room; 2s. 6d.). "A good sketch of Methodist History with which every student ought to be acquainted."

"**The Connexional Economy of Wesleyan Methodism.**" By Dr. Rigg. 3s. 6d.

"**Church Organisation.**" By Dr. Rigg, 1891. 7s. 6d.

2. *Works on the Special Business of Church Meetings*—

(*a*) **The Conference.**—Simon's "**Summary of Methodist Law and Discipline.**" (6s.) Section on "The Conference"; supplemented by the "Revised Regulations adapted to the changed order of Conference Sessions" in the Minutes of Conference, 1902, pages 523–527.

(*b*) *The Synod.*—"**Order and Form of Business**" (New Edition, 1903 ; 9d.).

(*c*) *The Circuit.*—"**Superintendent's Handbook.**" By the Rev. James E. Hargreaves. 1s. net.

3. *Works on the Duties of Ministers and Office-Bearers*—

(*a*) *Ministers.*—"**The Large Minutes.**"

(*b*) *Stewards.*—"**The Duties of Stewards.**" By the Rev. Edward Workman. 6d.

(*c*) *Leaders.*—"**Rules of Society and Introduction to the Class-book.**"

"**A Manual of Instruction and Advice for Class Leaders.**" By Rev. John S. Simon. (2s.) Prepared by order of the Conference.

(*d*) *Local Preachers.*—"**Lay Preachers' Handbook.**" By C. O. Eldridge, B.A. 2s. "**A History of Lay Preaching.**" By John Telford, B.A. 2s. 6d.

(*e*) *Wesley Guild Workers.*—"**The Wesley Guild Manual.**" 8d. net.

4. *Reference Books and Works of Interest on Special Topics*—

"**A Summary of Methodist Law and Discipline.**" By the Rev. John S. Simon, 1896. (Second Edition, 1898 ; 6s.) Every minister receives at his ordination a copy of this book, which has taken the place of the "Large Minutes." The document upon which the "Summary" is founded was drawn up in 1797, and contained the Rules which were believed to be "essential to the existence of Methodism." The original document was signed by Dr. Coke as president, Samuel Bradburn, secretary, and by a number of other preachers. Mr. Simon's book is a codification of the rules which have been passed up to the year 1898. It is a book of standard reference on all questions relating to the Society, the Circuit, the Minister, the Synod, and the Conference, and it is "our only official code of laws."

"The Constitution and Polity of Wesleyan Methodism." By Dr. Williams. Revised by Dr. Waller. This is a work more expository and historical. It explains the meaning of our institutions, and traces their growth from stage to stage.

"Essay on the Constitution of Wesleyan Methodism." By Dr. Beecham. (Out of print.) Of this, Mr. Simon writes: "There is one book dealing with the principles of our government which every young minister should read. It is Dr. Beecham's "Essay on the Constitution of Wesleyan Methodism." Francis A. West introduced it to my notice when he was my chairman. He said, 'Wear your coat until it is green, but get that book.' After many years of study of Methodism I still hold Dr. Beecham's Essay in the highest esteem."

"The Constitution and Discipline of Wesleyan Methodism." By George Turner. (Out of print.)

"A little-known and admirable volume . . . written shortly after the events of 1835."

Grindrod's "Compendium of the Laws and Regulations of Wesleyan Methodism." (Out of print.) "If a man wishes," says Mr. Simon, "to do his work thoroughly, he will read Grindrod's 'Compendium,' noting as he does so the changes in the Constitution that have taken place."

Peirce's "Ecclesiastical Principles and Polity of the Wesleyan Methodists." (15s.) "I also like," writes Mr. Simon, "to consult this work. You get in Peirce an historical sketch interwoven with the regulations, and can see the progress of legislation from the earliest Methodist times. I am afraid that the book has fallen out of use, but its value is great."

"The First Volume of the Minutes of Conference." (Vol. i. 8vo, 8s.) Revised by Dr. Osborn, and published in 1862. "Most interesting as showing the foundation lines upon which our Constitution rests. Special note should be taken of the fact that the 1862 edition is the best."

"Handy Digest of Wesleyan Rules." (Out of print.) By Charles Povah. "It served a good purpose in its day; but as it was published in 1883, many changes have occurred since then."

"Ross's Telescope." (1s.) A handy chart, showing at a glance the growth of Methodism, and the dates of the chief events in our history since the death of Wesley.

"Handbook and Index to the Minutes of Conference." (5s.) By Charles E. Wansbrough. "Indispensable," says Mr. Simon, "to a man who possesses a complete edition of the Minutes of Conference. It is a most painstaking and exact book, valued by every one who has to do hard work on the regulations of the Conference. I was much helped by it when I had to codify a hundred years of Conference legislation."

"London Quarterly Review." (2s. 6d. each No. Some out of print.) Articles by the Rev. John S. Simon on the Constitutional History of Methodism from 1739–1835. The articles will be found in Jan. 1884; Oct. 1884; Oct. 1885; Oct. 1886; July 1887; July 1888; April 1890; Oct. 1890; Jan. 1892; April 1892; Oct. 1892; and Oct. 1893. Mention ought also to be made of two articles in the *Wesleyan Methodist Magazine*, July and August 1887, giving a sketch of the Methodist Constitution as it appeared in 1810.

Mr. Simon also says, "The man who would understand the Constitutional History of Methodism must give his days and nights to the study of piles of pamphlets. We have, in the Didsbury College Library, a valuable collection. But I am afraid that such thorough study of the subject is rare."

It may be hoped that this outline of study will make a thorough knowledge of the growth of our Church more general in the future.

7. THE SISTER CHURCHES OF METHODISM

The books named under this head have all been suggested by either the Editor or Book Steward of each of the Churches concerned. The affiliated Methodist Conferences are not mentioned separately, as their polity is practically the same as our own. In every case the books selected are, as far as possible, brief, and non-controversial in character. The study of them would greatly help to an understanding of Greater Methodism.

1. The Methodist Episcopal Churches of America.

> "**Methodist Constitutions and Charters.**" — (Eaton & Mains, New York; $1.) A volume of 316 pages, containing the charters and constitutions of all the chief organisations in connection with the Methodist Episcopal Churches of America, both North and South.

> "**The Discipline of the Methodist Episcopal Church.**"—(Eaton & Mains, New York.)

2. The Canadian Methodist Church.

> "**The Doctrine and Discipline of the Methodist Church.**"—(Methodist Book and Publishing House, Toronto; leather, $1.)

> "**Centennial of Canadian Methodism.**" —(Toronto; $1.25.)

3. The Primitive Methodist Connexion.

> "**Handbook of Primitive Methodist Church Principles.**"—(Primitive Methodist Publishing House; 4d. and 6d.)

4. The United Methodist Free Churches.

"Historic Sketches of Free Methodism."
By Joseph Kirsop (Andrew Crombie; 1s.).

"Free Methodist Manual."—(Andrew Crombie.)

5. The Methodist New Connexion.

"The Centenary Volume," 1797–1897. 1s. 6d.

"Handbook for the Methodist New Connexion." By W. J. Townsend, D.D. 1s. 6d.

6. The Bible Christians.

"Digest of Rules and Regulations."— (Bible Christian Book-Room; 1s. 6d.)

7. The Calvinistic Methodists.

"The Confession of Faith."—(Hughes & Sons, Wrexham; 6d., 1s., and 1s. 6d.)

"Welsh Calvinistic Methodism." By Rev. W. Williams (Hughes & Sons, Wrexham; 2s.).

8. METHODIST SONG

This most interesting topic, the importance of which is felt by every student of Wesley, whether he approaches the subject from the theological, the historical, or the biographical side, deserves much broader treatment than it has yet received. There is a large field for new workers. For the following very valuable notes I am indebted to Mr. J. T. Lightwood,

of Lytham, who has a knowledge of both the hymnology and psalmody of Methodism which very few
possess.

METHODIST HYMNS AND TUNES.

Notes by Mr. J. T. Lightwood.

A. Hymns.

The study of hymnology has been taken up so
thoroughly during the last few years that the field of
original research in this subject, especially from a
Methodist standpoint, is somewhat limited. However, for the great majority who have neither time nor
opportunity for original study, there is a fine collection
of works setting forth the history of all the hymns in
current use in the Churches, together with much information about the writers. For Methodist hymnology
the first place must undoubtedly be given to the late
G. J. Stevenson, whose **"Methodist Hymn=
Book"** (Kelly; 5s.) contains a detailed account of all
the hymns in the 1875 edition of the Hymn-Book.
This book is specially adapted for the use of teachers in
the senior classes of our Sunday schools, and also for
leaders and local preachers. It contains a wealth of
illustrative anecdote showing the circumstances under
which the hymns have been used on special occasions,
and the whole work is a wonderful testimony to the
value and popularity of the Methodist hymns. It
should be understood at once that the phrase, "Methodist hymns," does not mean hymns by Methodists, but
those in general use by Methodists. The Methodist

Church did not produce a nineteenth-century hymn-writer of the first rank, but it is the glory of our Churches that when we reach our hymn-singing, sectarianism vanishes.

Stevenson also published an earlier work in 1869, **"The Methodist Hymn=Book and its Associa=tions,"** a second edition of which was published in 1871, but which is now out of print. This work had special reference to the book then in use, but it was allowed to go out of print when the 1875 hymn-book appeared.

There are four other works referring to the hymn-book in use in the earlier part of the nineteenth century, all by Wesleyan ministers.

1. **Wesleyan Hymnology.** By Burgess.
2. **Original Titles of Hymns.** By Kirk.
3. **Round and through the Wesleyan Hymn=Book.** By Ward.
4. **Two Lectures on the Wesleyan Hymn=Book.** By Heaton.

Out of print.

These may occasionally be met with in the second-hand book shops, or consulted in the reference libraries of our largest towns. Burgess's work is critical, the others dwell principally on the historical aspects of the hymns.

Two works by the **Rev. S. W. Christophers** should by all means be consulted. His **" Poets of Methodism "** (Houghton & Co.) is a most interesting work, and furnishes ample proof that if Methodism has not produced many hymn-writers, she has brought out poets of great excellence. This is probably the only book in existence that deals in detail with the poetical works of such well-known men as Smetham, B. Gough, John Harris the Cornish miner, with T. Garland and Richard Rodda, also of Cornish birth, and many others. This work is indispensable to a lover of Methodist literature.

Another work by Christophers is called "**Hymn= writers and their Hymns**" (S. W. Partridge; 3s. 6d.). This is of a more general character, but the plan on which it is laid out is excellent, and each chapter treats of a set of well-known hymns on a particular subject. Christophers was a vivid and interesting writer, though sometimes perhaps a little diffuse, and his books should not be allowed to fall into disuse.

Let us now consider the works on hymnology by writers outside the Methodist Church. One of the best available books on the subject is "**The Hymn= Lover**," by **Garrett Horder** (Curwen & Sons; 5s.). This book contains a capital estimate of hymns and hymn-writers, and the author's criticisms are singularly apt and fair. Moreover, the work possesses considerable literary style, and its author is a recognised authority on the subject. Mr. Horder has also issued a most valuable and complete collection of hymns under the title of "**Worship Song**" (Elliot Stock; 2s. 6d.), which is largely used in Congregational Churches.

The most recent popular work on this subject is "**Famous Hymns**," by F. A. Jones (Hodder & Stoughton; 5s.). It contains a few facsimiles and several excellent portraits. The subject-matter is put together in an interesting manner, and the book could be recommended more cordially if it did not contain some silly anecdotes of mythical origin, the recital of which is bound to impair the value of the hymns to which they allude. This book is evidently the result of long and diligent research, and the author brings to light many new facts.

The standard book of reference on this subject is, and will be for many years to come, the monumental work by the **Rev. Dr. Julian,** the "**Dictionary of Hymnology.**" (42s.) It may be consulted in most large reference libraries, but is rather a book for special reference for the student, and not likely to be of much use to the ordinary reader.

A very useful little book is "**Hymns that have Helped,**" compiled by W. T. Stead (*Review of Reviews* Office ; 2d.). It is a double number of the "Penny Poet" series, and furnishes some interesting information not found elsewhere. It also contains some very fine hymns that are not usually found together under one cover.

"**Lyric Studies**" (J. Toulson), by Dorricott and Collins, is a useful companion to the Primitive Methodist Hymnal of 1887. The first part is biographical, while the second contains useful notes on each hymn.

It is well known to what extent our Hymnody is enriched by translations from the German. One of the best-known translators is **Miss Winkworth**, who has also written an excellent manual, entitled "**Christian Singers of Germany**" (Macmillan

& Co.). A most interesting account of hymns belonging to the earlier periods of the Christian Church is "**Te Deum Laudamus**," by **Mrs. Rundle Charles** (S.P.C.K). These last two works possess the additional advantage of being written in good, well-chosen language, a remark which also applies in a high degree to **Rev. F. W. Macdonald's** able study of "**Latin Hymn=writers and their Hymns,**" published by Rev. C. H. Kelly; 2s. 6d.

While this list could of course be considerably extended, it contains most of the principal works on hymns and hymn-writers that are published at a price within the reach of all (except Julian's). One other book should, however, be mentioned—the "**Life of John Ellerton**" (S.P.C.K.). This contains an interesting account of the life and labours of one of the finest of modern hymnists, and at the end there is a collection of essays and biographical sketches by Ellerton, which are of considerable value.

B. Tunes.

Although hymn-singing has always been a special feature in the services of the Methodist Church, it is a remarkable fact that scarcely anything is known about the history of the tunes or the lives of the composers. It may be stated at once that there is no special literature on the subject of Methodist music, and its history is yet to be written. There is here an immense field of work for any who are fond of Church music and singing to work in, and if the Wesley Guilds would initiate some scheme of this kind, they would be rendering invaluable service. Early in 1903 a circular letter appeared in many of the religious papers appealing for information on this subject, and the number of letters received in reply showed how great was the desire to know more about the tunes and their composers. But although Methodist music has not yet received the attention it deserves, there is a certain amount of literature on the history of Church music. One of the most readable books of this nature is "**Studies in Worship Music**" (Curwen & Sons; 1st Series, 5s.; 2nd Series, 2s. 6d.). Two series have been issued, but the first is the more interesting and important. It is by Mr. J. Spencer Curwen, and he has spared no pains to make his book as complete as possible. The chief feature of the work is a series of chapters devoted to the history of the music of various Nonconformist Churches, and the chapter devoted to Methodist music is very interesting.

A very useful book for ministers, local preachers, organists, and all who have authority over the music of the Church, is "**United Praise**," by F. G. Edwards (Curwen & Sons; 3s. 6d.). It contains chapters on chanting, hymn-singing, the special uses of music in Nonconformist churches, and other allied subjects. Mr. Edwards also wrote a few short biographies of hymn-tune composers (Gauntlett, Dykes, Monk, etc.), which were inserted in a work called the "**Romance of Psalter and Hymnal**," by Rev. R. E. Welsh, M.A., and F. G. Edwards (Hodder & Stoughton; 6s.).

The book as a whole, however, cannot be recommended, as the non-musical part is very poor and "scrappy."

There is a good article on "Congregational Singing" in a little book by the Rev. H. C. Shuttleworth, called **"The Place of Music in Public Worship"** (Elliot Stock). The same publisher has also issued a work called **"Chapters on Church Music,"** by Rev. R. B. Daniel. It is a useful and interesting book, but the subject is treated entirely from an Anglican point of view. There are very few works on eighteenth-century Church music, for the simple reason that there was none in the proper sense of the term. Several pamphlets were issued, chiefly by clergymen, finding fault with the deplorable state of music in the Church of England. John Wesley makes very few references to music in his "Journals," but his introduction to a tune-book issued under his direction, called **"Sacred Melody,"** might be read with advantage in Methodist chapels (and elsewhere) every now and then.

There are various articles on Church music, and on the history and writers of certain hymn-tunes, scattered through the musical and other magazines, but it is impossible to specify these. There is, however, a connected history of the use of Methodist music appearing at intervals in the **"Proceedings of the Wesley Historical Society."**

Nor is the literature of eighteenth-century music generally much richer. True, the period is embraced in the large musical histories to be found in the libraries, but we look in vain for a readable book on the times when not only Handel and other foreigners flourished in England, but when also Croft, Carey, Arne, Nares, Jackson, and others were popular composers. Until such a work is forthcoming, biographies of individuals must suffice, and an interesting and generally well-written series is "**The Great Musicians**" (Low, Marston, & Co.; 14 vols., 2s. 6d. each). The volumes dealing with Handel, and with "English Church Composers," are suitable. The story of Charles Wesley's two precocious sons is told in his "Journals," and it contains references to contemporary musicians.

The student who wishes to go further into the matter may be referred to Davey's "**History of English Music**" (Curwen & Sons). The work as a whole is good, and many parts are very readable.

9. METHODIST ANTIQUARIAN STUDY

"**Proceedings of the Wesley Historical Society.**" Three volumes published, the fourth commenced. The Wesley Historical Society was instituted to promote the study of our Church and its growth. Anyone interested in the subject may join, at an annual subscription of 5s. Working members who engage to do actual research, pay 2s. 6d. per annum.

Among the most important numbers of the Proceedings yet issued are—

"*The Bennet Minutes,*" 1744–48, referred to in the chapter on "The Conference."

"Published Biographies of John Wesley." An invaluable collation of Wesley's Lives, Histories, Essays, and Pamphlets, by the Rev. Richard Green.

The secretaries of the Society are the Revs. M. Riggall and J. W. Crake.

"Wesley Bibliography." By the Rev. Richard Green. (2s. 6d. net.) "An exact account of all the publications issued by the brothers Wesley . . . with descriptive and illustrative notes." Indispensable to anyone engaging in Wesley research, and suggesting a score of pathways as yet scarcely trodden.

Among subjects the fringe of which has scarcely been touched by previous publications may be named :—

Wesley's Character as Illustrated in his Correspondence.

Wesley's Place in Literature.

Wesley's Intercourse with the Men of the Eighteenth Century.

Wesley and Children.

Wesley as a Pioneer in Social and Philanthropic Enterprise.

Wesley and the Industrial Revolution.

Wesley's Writings in the *Arminian Magazine.*

Printed by
MORRISON & GIBB LIMITED
Edinburgh

CHARLES H. KELLY'S PUBLICATIONS.

Wesley Studies. A Reprint of the Articles that appeared in the Bi-Centenary Numbers of the *Wesleyan Methodist Magazine* and the *Methodist Recorder.* Demy 8vo.

John Wesley's First Sermons. Reproduced in Facsimile, hitherto unpublished ; and other First Things in the Life of the Father of Methodism. Printed on art paper, demy 8vo, white leatherette, 1s. net.

John Wesley's Journal. Popular Edition Condensed. With Introduction by Rev. W. L. WATKINSON. In Two Volumes. Small demy 8vo (size 8 by 5½ inches), cloth, gilt top, 3s. 6d. each.

John Wesley's Journal. Condensed Edition in One Volume. Fcap. 8vo, cloth, gilt lettered, gilt top, 2s. ; leather, whole gilt edges, gilt lettered, 3s.

The Seekers. A Romance of Modern Methodism. By Rev. W. KINGSCOTE GREENLAND (W. Scott King). Twenty-four full-page Illustrations. Crown 8vo, art vellum, gilt top, 3s. 6d. This Tale appeared in the *Wesleyan Methodist Magazine* for 1902 under the title of "Pilgrims of the Night."

The Rockingstone Schoolmaster. By HARRY LINDSAY, Author of "Methodist Idylls." Crown 8vo, art vellum, gilt top, 3s. 6d.

How David Hill followed Christ. A Biography. By JANE E. HELLIER. With Portrait. Crown 8vo, cloth, 2s. 6d.

New Volume by Rev. JOSEPH DAWSON.

Pictures of Christ framed in Prayers. A Unique and Suggestive rendering of the Gospel Story in Verse, with appropriate Scripture Passages and Prayers, forming at once a Life of our Lord and a Text-book of Devotion. By Rev. JOSEPH DAWSON. Printed in Colours, with decorated borders on art paper. Art vellum, red edges, 3s. ; paste grain, limp, round corners, gilt edges, 4s. 6d. ; Persian calf limp, round corners, red under gilt edges, 5s. 6d. ; Morocco limp, round corners, red under gilt edges, 7s. 6d.

The Bane and the Antidote, and other Sermons. By Rev. W. L. WATKINSON. Third Thousand. Post 8vo, 3s. 6d.

My Jewels, and other Sermons. By Rev. RICHARD ROBERTS, Author of "The Living One." Crown 8vo, 3s. 6d.

Makers of Methodism. By Rev. W. H. WITHROW, D D. Illustrated. Crown 8vo, 2s. 6d.

The Art of Noble Living. By Rev. R. P. DOWNES, LL.D. Second Thousand. Crown 8vo, art linen, gilt top, 3s. 6d. net. May also be had full gilt back, uniform with "Woman" and "Pure Pleasures." Price 3s. 9d. net.

The Mangle House. By JOHN ACKWORTH, Author of "Clog Shop Chronicles," etc. Second Thousand. Crown 8vo, art linen, gilt top, 3s. 6d.

LONDON : CHARLES H. KELLY, 2, CASTLE STREET, CITY ROAD ; AND 26, PATERNOSTER ROW, E.C.

THE WESLEY GUILD LIBRARY.

Crown 12mo, art linen, gilt top.

A Young Man's Bookshelf. By Rev. GEORGE JACKSON, B.A.,
of Edinburgh. Third Thousand. 2s. 6d.

The *Bookman* says : "Excellent advice to young men on reading, with some sound criticism of modern literature, examinations of special books, and hints for self-culture."

FOR YOUNG WOMEN.

Life on High Levels. Familiar Talks on the Conduct of Life.
By MARGARET E. SANGSTER. Second Thousand. 2s. 6d.

The *Sheffield Independent* says : "This book may be placed in the hands of thoughtful young people with the fullest confidence that they will be helped by its wholesome counsels. Practical good sense is the substance of the work."

Thinking About It. Thoughts on Religion for Young Men and
Women. By Rev. A. H. WALKER, B.A. Second Thousand. 2s. 6d.

"Mr. Walker is a gifted and cultured advocate of the highest of all causes. These addresses, both for their vigour and sincere earnestness, will be sure to claim the particular attention of readers. His appeal is put in clear, terse language, and the sympathy he shows for young people with honest difficulties should secure their attention."—*Western Daily Press.*

Depth and Power of the Christian Faith. By Rev. ARTHUR
HOYLE. Second Thousand. 1s. 6d.

"Breezy, manful, strong in exposition and appeal, they will be sure to secure a large audience."—*Sword and Trowel.*

BOOKS FOR THE HEART.

Printed on antique wove paper. Fcap. 8vo, cloth boards, gilt top, 2s. 6d. each.

The Confessions of St. Augustine.

"No cheap edition of 'The Confessions' that we know of can be at all compared with this in beauty of outward form. Type, paper, and binding are alike irreproachable."—*Church Times.*

Grace Abounding to the Chief of Sinners. By JOHN BUNYAN.

Dr. ALEXANDER WHYTE, Author of "Bunyan's Characters," writes : "My best thanks for your beautiful 'Grace Abounding.' Go on with such good work."

The Religious Affections. By JONATHAN EDWARDS.

"My heart bounded when I saw 'The Religious Affections' announced under your editorship, and so cheap too. . . . Many whose blessing is worth earning will bless you for Edwards' masterpiece in this beautiful shape."—ALEXANDER WHYTE, Edinburgh.

The Journal of John Woolman. With an Appreciation by
JOHN GREENLEAF WHITTIER.

"The Journal is quaint reading and the language is charmingly piquant."—*Bookman.*

"To read his quaint, gracious jottings is to breathe an air of pious peace, and sturdy devotion to practical righteousness. For devotional stimulus and preparation for personal communion with God this will be a sweet aid."—*Sword and Trowel.*

Quiet Hours. By JOHN PULSFORD, D.D.

"It is a casket of jewels from which flash the many-coloured rays of well-cut gems. It is essentially a volume for thoughtful men and women of reverent mind, and to them the pages often conned will be ever fresh."—*Rock.*

LONDON : CHARLES H. KELLY, 2, CASTLE STREET, CITY ROAD ;
AND 26, PATERNOSTER ROW, E.C.